FREIDA BAILEY

# MASTERING STRESS

*Proven Techniques, Natural Solutions and Effective Strategies for Coping, Preventing, and Thriving in Life*

# Contents

# 1

## INTRODUCTION

In today's fast-paced world, stress has become a constant companion, hurting us physically, emotionally, and psychologically. Stress manifests itself in a variety of ways, from professional responsibilities to personal pressures, and it has a tremendous impact on our well-being.

But, amidst the confusion, there is a way to comprehend and manage stress. Welcome to this path of self-discovery and empowerment. This comprehensive guide delves into the complex web of stress, including its various forms, symptoms, and underlying causes. We investigate the various coping tactics, ranging from ancient mindfulness practices to cutting-edge cognitive-behavioral treatments, all designed to provide you with the tools you need to thrive in the face of hardship.

Drawing on cutting-edge research and timeless wisdom, we reveal the subtle dance between stress and our lifestyles, emphasizing the significance of self-care, social support, and resilience in our pursuit of overall well-being. Whether you're a seasoned warrior dealing with chronic stress or a beginner looking for prevention strategies, this book will serve as a beacon of knowledge and a road map to recover control of your life.

## Understanding Stress: An Overview

Stress is a common term that affects everyone at some point in their lives. It's an unavoidable aspect of the human experience, but the consequences can be profound and far-reaching. Stress manifests itself in a variety of ways, from fluttering nervousness before a job interview to the heavier weight of financial anxieties. But what is stress and how does it affect us?

At its foundation, stress is the body's natural reaction to perceived dangers or challenges. It's our primordial instincts taking over, preparing us to fight, flee, or freeze in the face of danger. This "fight-or-flight" response, defined by physiologist Walter Cannon in the early twentieth century, is a basic survival mechanism that is firmly embedded in our evolutionary history. When we are confronted with a stressor, such as a looming deadline, a contentious encounter, event an unexpected loss, our systems respond by producing a cascade of chemicals, including cortisol and adrenaline, to mobilise resources and increase awareness.

## Types of Stress

Stress is not a single entity, but rather a complex phenomenon with several shades and intensities. Stress is generally classified into three types: acute stress, chronic stress, and episodic acute stress.

**Acute stress:** This is the most prevalent type of stress, caused by short-term stressors such as a traffic jam, a heated dispute, or an impending deadline. Acute stress is often manageable and normally goes away as the stressor is handled source removed.

**Chronic stress:** unlike acute stress, is long-lasting and results from repeated exposure to stressors such as financial challenges, dysfunctional relationships, or continuing health issues. Chronic stress can have a substantial impact on both physical and mental health, increasing the risk of hypertension, anxiety disorders, and depression.

**Episodic acute stress:** Characterized by numerous bouts of acute stress and is typically seen in those who live chaotic or disorganized lives. They frequently handle many stresses at once, ranging from professional demands to home issues, resulting in a condition of constant tension and overwhelm.

## Physiological Responses to Stress

When confronted with a stressor, our bodies undergo a sequence of physiological changes that prepare us for action. The hypothalamus, a small brain region, triggers the stress response by signaling the release of chemicals from the adrenal glands, which are placed atop the kidneys. These hormones, particularly cortisol and adrenaline, rush into the bloodstream, readying the body for action.

## Physiologically, stress causes a cascade of effects

- **Increased Heart Rate and Blood Pressure:** Adrenaline causes the heart to beat faster and blood vessels to constrict, ensuring that oxygen and nutrients reach essential organs quickly.
- **Heightened Alertness and Sensory Perception:** Cortisol improves sensory awareness and cognitive function, increasing our focus and vigilance in the face of danger.
- **Suppressed Immune Function:** Prolonged stress can weaken the immune system, leaving us more vulnerable to infections and illnesses.
- **Disrupted Digestive Function:** Stress hormones can alter digestive functions, causing symptoms such as nausea, stomach cramps, and diarrhea.

While these physiological changes are temporary adaptations, prolonged activation of the stress response can hurt human health, contributing to a variety of chronic problems ranging from cardiovascular disease to autoimmune disorders.

# The Psychological Effects of Stress

Beyond its bodily effects, stress has a significant impact on our mental and emotional health. Stress may permeate every part of our life, influencing our thoughts, feelings, and behaviours in significant ways.

**Cognitive Effects:** Stress can affect our cognitive skills, making it difficult to concentrate, retrieve memories, and make decisions. We may find ourselves dwelling on worst-case scenarios or unable to concentrate in the middle of a barrage of distractions.

**Emotional Disturbances:** Stress can cause a range of feelings, including anxiety, anger, melancholy, and despair. We may feel on edge, awaiting the next disaster, or we may experience mood swings that leave us emotionally exhausted and depleted.

**Behavioral Changes:** Stress can cause major adjustments in our behaviors. Some people may utilize maladaptive coping techniques, such as substance addiction or compulsive behaviors, to get brief relief from their discomfort. Others may withdraw socially, seeking seclusion for self-preservation.

Navigating the complicated terrain of stress necessitates a holistic approach that considers both physiological and psychological aspects. We can begin to regain control of our lives and nurture a higher feeling of well-being by increasing our awareness of our stressors, creating adaptive coping mechanisms, and growing resilience in the face of adversity.

2

# CHAPTER ONE: TYPES OF STRESS

## Acute Stress

Stress manifests itself in a variety of ways in the human experience, each with its texture and intensity. Acute stress, sometimes compared to a sudden storm on the horizon, is one such manifestation a fleeting yet powerful force that can leave us disturbed and disoriented in its aftermath.

## Understanding Acute Stress

Acute stress is a type of stress that lasts only a short time and comes on suddenly. It usually occurs in response to urgent stressors or threats, such as a near-miss vehicle accident, a surprise presentation at work, or an unexpected confrontation with a loved one. Unlike chronic stress, which lasts for a long time, acute stress is temporary and goes away once the stressor is handled or removed.

## Triggers for Acute Stress

Acute stress can be caused by a variety of situations, both positive and negative, that disrupt our sense of balance and test our coping abilities. Common triggers include:

- **Life Events:** Major life transitions, like as relocating to a new place, starting a new job, or losing a loved one, can cause acute stress reactions as we navigate uncharted territory and adjust to the upheaval.
- **Interpersonal Conflicts:** Conflictual relationships with family members, friends, or colleagues can cause acute stress responses, such as annoyance, rage, or helplessness, as we deal with interpersonal tensions and misunderstandings.
- **Work-related Pressures:** Work-related pressures include deadlines, performance assessments, and high-stakes presentations, all of which can cause acute stress reactions, fuelling a sense of urgency and anxiety as we strive to meet expectations and achieve outcomes.
- **Environmental Stressors:** Natural disasters, traffic congestion, and noisy surroundings can all cause acute stress reactions as we negotiate bad situations and adjust to the challenges given by our environment.

## Physiological Responses to Acute Stress

When confronted with an acute stressor, our bodies initiate a quick and coordinated response that prepares us for action. This "fight-or-flight" response, organized by the sympathetic nervous system and the production of stress hormones such as adrenaline and cortisol, causes a series of physiological changes:

- **Increased Heart Rate and Blood Pressure:** Adrenaline causes the heart to beat faster and blood vessels to constrict, ensuring that oxygen and nutrients reach essential organs quickly.
- **Heightened Alertness and Vigilance:** Cortisol increases alertness and vigi-

lance by improving sensory perception and cognitive function, sharpening attention and readiness to respond to perceived dangers.

- **Activation of the HPA Axis:** The hypothalamic-pituitary-adrenal (HPA) axis, a complex interaction of hormonal signals involving the hypothalamus, pituitary gland, and adrenal glands, is activated, resulting in the production of cortisol to mobilize energy stores while suppressing non-essential body activities.
- **Suppression of Digestive and Immune Systems:** During acute stress, resources are shifted away from non-essential body systems such as digestion and immunity, focusing energy towards immediate survival demands.

While these physiological changes are beneficial in the short term, persistent activation of the stress response can be detrimental to human health, increasing the risk of cardiovascular disease, gastrointestinal disorders, and immunological dysfunction.

## Coping strategies for acute stress

In the face of severe stress, developing good coping techniques is critical for controlling our reactions and building resilience. Here are some practical ways to manage acute stress:

- **Deep Breathing and Relaxation:** To generate a state of peace and relaxation amid a stressful situation, do deep breathing exercises, progressive muscle relaxation, or mindfulness meditation.
- **Cognitive Reframing:** Challenge negative thought patterns and catastrophic thinking by framing stressful situations in a more balanced and helpful manner. Focus on solutions rather than problems, and create a resilient and optimistic mindset.
- **Social Support:** Reach out to friends, family members, or trusted colleagues for emotional support and advice. Sharing your issues with others can provide you with validation, empathy, and practical help when you

need it.

- **Physical Activity:** Engage in regular physical activity, such as brisk walking, jogging, or yoga, to relieve tension and encourage the secretion of endorphins, which are natural mood-boosting substances that offset the effects of stress.
- **Time Management:** Break down large projects into smaller, more manageable pieces, and prioritize your activities according to urgency and importance. Set reasonable goals and deadlines, and assign tasks as needed to avoid feeling overwhelmed.
- **Self-Care Practices:** Prioritise self-care activities that nourish your body, mind, and soul, such as obtaining enough sleep, eating healthy food, and engaging in hobbies or activities that make you happy and fulfilled.

# Chronic Stress

Chronic stress is a long-term and chronic form of stress caused by continual exposure to stressors or difficulties, both internal and external, that outweigh our coping abilities. Chronic stress, as opposed to acute stress, which is short-lived and usually dissipates once the stressor is eliminated, lasts for a lengthy period and has a long-term impact on our physiological and psychological health.

## Causes of Chronic Stress

Chronic stress can be caused by a multitude of reasons, including the environment, interpersonal relationships, internal issues, and unresolved trauma. Some common causes of persistent stress are:

- **Work-related Pressures:** High-pressure work environments, tight deadlines, and job instability can all contribute to chronic stress reactions as people deal with the constant demands of the workplace and the looming threat of burnout.
- **Financial Strain:** Financial strain can cause chronic stress responses as

people try to make ends meet and protect their financial future.

- **Relationship Strain:** Dysfunctional relationships, marital problems, and social isolation can all add to chronic stress, as people deal with emotional upheaval and interpersonal issues that weaken their sense of belonging and support.
- **Health Challenges:** Chronic illnesses, persistent pain, and disability can all increase stress levels as people deal with the physical and emotional demands of managing their health problems and navigating the healthcare system.
- **Traumatic Experiences:** Past trauma, abuse, or unfavorable childhood experiences can leave long-term psychological scars, predisposing people to chronic stress reactions as they deal with the aftermath of trauma and the struggle of healing and rehabilitation.

## Symptoms of chronic stress

Chronic stress can take many forms, hurting both our physical and emotional health. Some common signs of chronic stress are:

- **Physical Symptoms:** Chronic stress can cause headaches, muscle tension, digestive issues, exhaustion, and sleep difficulties. Prolonged activation of the stress response can also lead to the development or worsening of chronic health issues like hypertension, cardiovascular disease, and autoimmune disorders.
- **Emotional Disturbances:** Chronic stress can hurt our emotional health, causing symptoms such as impatience, mood swings, anxiety, sadness, and feelings of overwhelm or powerlessness. Individuals may experience emotional numbness or detachment as a coping tactic to avoid the intensity of their emotions.
- **Cognitive Impairments:** Chronic stress can impede cognitive function, making it difficult to concentrate, retain memories, and make decisions. Individuals may have cognitive distortions or negative thought patterns, which exacerbate feelings of self-doubt, pessimism, or hopelessness.

- **Behavioral Changes:** Chronic stress can have a tremendous impact on our behavior, leading to maladaptive coping methods such as substance misuse, compulsive behaviors, overeating, and social disengagement. Individuals may struggle to maintain healthy lifestyle choices such as regular exercise, balanced nutrition, and appropriate sleep, worsening the stress-disfunction loop.

## Coping Strategies for Chronic Stress

In the face of persistent stress, developing good coping techniques is critical for controlling our reactions and building resilience. While there is no one-size-fits-all answer, the tactics listed below may help individuals negotiate the problems of chronic stress:

1. **Stress Management Techniques:** To generate a sense of calm and relaxation in the middle of chronic stress, try deep breathing exercises, progressive muscle relaxation, or mindfulness meditation.
2. **Cognitive Restructuring:** Challenge negative thought patterns and cognitive distortions by framing stressful situations in a more balanced and helpful manner. Practice self-compassion and create a resilient, optimistic outlook.
3. **Social Support:** Seek social support from friends, family members, or support groups who can offer empathy, affirmation, and practical aid during times of need. Encourage connections and interactions that provide a sense of belonging and community.
4. **Healthy Lifestyle Habits:** Put self-care activities that nourish your body, mind, and spirit first, such as regular exercise, balanced nutrition, enough sleep, and relaxation techniques. Avoid unhealthy coping techniques like binge drinking, smoking, or overeating.
5. **Professional treatment:** If chronic stress is interfering with your quality of life and functioning, do not hesitate to seek professional treatment. A therapist, counselor, or mental health professional can offer you support, advice, and evidence-based therapies to help you cope with chronic stress

and build resilience.

# Environmental Stressors

Environmental stressors are a wide range of external stimuli or conditions in our environment that put a strain on our physical, mental, or emotional well-being. These stressors can come from natural or man-made causes and vary greatly in severity, duration, and impact. While some environmental stressors are obvious and instantly noticeable, others may work more silently, gradually building over time to damage our health and vitality.

## Types of Environmental Stressors

Environmental stressors are divided into numerous groups based on their causes, characteristics, and effects. Some frequent environmental stressors include:

1. **Physical Environment:** Noise pollution, air pollution, temperature extremes, and natural disasters are all examples of the physical environment. Physical environmental stresses can interrupt our sensory experiences, jeopardize our physical health, and cause stress responses in the body.

2. **Social Environment:** The social environment includes interpersonal relationships, social dynamics, and cultural standards that influence our interactions and experiences. Social stressors such as loneliness, discrimination, bullying, and interpersonal disagreements can all damage our sense of belonging and support.

3. **Work Environment:** The work environment includes job demands, work-related pressures, organizational culture, and job instability. Work-related stressors, such as a heavy workload, time constraints, role uncertainty, or a lack of autonomy, can all contribute to burnout, exhaustion, and mental health issues.

**4. Digital Environment:** In the digital age, our interactions with technology and digital devices have created a new set of stresses. Information overload, constant connectedness, digital distractions, and cyberbullying are all potential sources of disruption to our attention, sleep patterns, and mental health.

**5. Built Environment:** The built environment refers to the physical infrastructure and design of our surroundings, such as buildings, transit systems, and city planning. Overcrowding, traffic congestion, poor infrastructure, and a lack of green space can all lead to feelings of claustrophobia, social isolation, and environmental stress.

## Effects of Environmental Stressors

Environmental stressors have a wide-ranging and complex impact on human health and well-being, influencing persons in physical, mental, and emotional realms. Common effects of environmental stresses include:

- **Physical Health Effects:** Environmental stressors can cause several physical health issues, such as cardiovascular disease, respiratory disorders, gastrointestinal problems, sleep abnormalities, and immunological dysfunction. Environmental contaminants, noise pollution, and temperature extremes can worsen pre-existing health issues and raise the risk of chronic diseases.
- **Mental Health Effects:** Environmental stresses can have a significant impact on mental health, including feelings of anxiety, sadness, and other mood disorders. Social stresses such as social isolation, discrimination, and bullying can lower self-esteem, sever social relationships, and increase the risk of mental illness.
- **Emotional Effects:** Environmental stressors can cause a variety of emotional responses, such as irritation, anger, grief, fear, and helplessness. Chronic exposure to environmental stressors can cause emotional tiredness, burnout, and a decreased ability to cope with daily obstacles.
- **Behavioral Effects:** Environmental stressors have a substantial impact

on our behaviors, decisions, and coping mechanisms. In reaction to environmental stressors, individuals may utilize maladaptive coping methods such as substance misuse, overeating, or social disengagement, aggravating the stress and dysfunction cycle.

## Strategies for mitigating environmental stressors

While we may not be able to control all environmental stressors, we can take action to reduce their impact and build resilience in the face of hardship. Here are some practical ways to manage environmental stressors:

- **Stress Management Techniques:** Deep breathing exercises, mindfulness meditation, or progressive muscular relaxation can help induce relaxation and lessen the physiological effects of environmental stresses on the body.
- **Environmental Modification:** Identify and address certain environmental stressors in your surroundings through changes or adjustments. This could involve utilizing noise-canceling headphones to filter out ambient noise, increasing indoor air quality using air purifiers or plants, or creating a peaceful and clutter-free office to minimise distractions.
- **Boundary Setting:** Set clear boundaries and limits to protect oneself from overexposure to environmental stresses. Learn to say no to activities or commitments that deplete your energy or cause stress, and instead prioritize activities that encourage relaxation, rejuvenation, and well-being.
- **Social Support:** Seek social support from friends, family members, or support groups who may offer understanding, affirmation, and practical help dealing with environmental pressures. Make connections and cultivate relationships that provide a sense of belonging and support.
- **Digital Detox:** Take regular vacations from technology and digital gadgets to unplug from the continual bombardment of information and stimulation. Set screen time limits, create tech-free zones in your house, and participate in offline activities that promote relaxation and connection with others.

· **Healthy Lifestyle Habits:** Put self-care activities that nourish your body, mind, and spirit first, such as regular exercise, balanced nutrition, enough sleep, and relaxation techniques. Maintain a healthy work-life balance and make time for hobbies, interests, and activities that make you happy and fulfilled.

3

# CHAPTER TWO: SIGNS AND SYMPTOMS OF STRESS

## Physical Symptoms

Stress frequently appears as a formidable companion in the complicated dance of human existence, leaving its imprint not only on our minds and emotions but also on our bodies. Physical stress symptoms are poignant reminders of the fundamental connection between mind and body, providing insights into the complex network of physiological responses that accompany our stressful experiences.

## Understanding Physical Symptoms of Stress

Physical symptoms of stress include a wide range of physiological feelings and disruptions that occur in response to the activation of the body's stress response system. These symptoms can take many different forms, from minor aches and pains to more severe manifestations that have a considerable influence on our everyday lives. While the particular symptoms experienced by each individual may differ, some frequent physical manifestations of stress include:

**1. Muscle Tension:** Stress can cause muscles to tighten, resulting in tightness, stiffness, or discomfort in the neck, shoulders, back, or jaw. Chronic muscle tension can cause headaches, migraines, and musculoskeletal diseases such as tension myalgia or temporomandibular joint dysfunction.

**2. Headaches:** Stress-induced tension and blood vessel constriction can cause headaches or migraines, which are characterized by throbbing or pulsating pain in the head. Stress headaches can be accompanied by symptoms such as sensitivity to light or noise, nausea, and vision problems.

**3. Gastrointestinal Disturbances:** Stress can alter digestive processes, causing symptoms like stomach cramps, bloating, diarrhea, constipation, and irritable bowel syndrome (IBS). Chronic stress can exacerbate gastrointestinal issues and cause digestive tract inflammation.

**4. Cardiovascular Symptoms:** Stress can raise heart rate, blood pressure, and stress hormone levels like adrenaline and cortisol, raising the risk of cardiovascular disorders like hypertension, palpitations, chest pain, and arrhythmias.

**5. Respiratory Symptoms:** Stress-induced sympathetic nervous system activation can cause rapid, shallow breathing or hyperventilation, worsening respiratory disorders including asthma or chronic obstructive pulmonary disease.

**6. Sleep Disturbances:** Stress can disturb sleep habits, making it harder to get asleep, stay asleep, or get enough restorative sleep. Stress can cause insomnia, nightmares, and frequent awakenings.

**7. Immune Suppression:** Prolonged stress can impair immune function, increasing susceptibility to infections, allergies, and autoimmune illnesses. Stress-induced immune response alterations can decrease the body's ability to protect itself against infections and increase inflammation.

## Impacts of Physical Symptoms of Stress

Physical symptoms of stress not only create discomfort and anxiety, but they can also have a significant impact on our general health and well-being. Chronic stress and its physical manifestations, if left untreated, can contribute to a variety of health issues and exacerbate pre-existing medical illnesses. Some common implications of bodily symptoms of stress are:

- **Chronic Health Conditions:** Prolonged activation of the stress response system increases the chance of acquiring chronic health problems such as hypertension, cardiovascular disease, gastrointestinal disorders, respiratory illnesses, and autoimmune disorders.
- **Pain and Discomfort:** Persistent muscle tension, headaches, and other stress-related physical symptoms can create chronic pain and discomfort, limiting daily activities and quality of life. Stress can increase chronic pain illnesses like fibromyalgia and tension headaches.
- **Sleep Disturbances:** Sleep disturbances caused by stress can affect cognitive performance, emotional control, and immune function, raising the risk of exhaustion, irritability, cognitive impairment, and sickness.
- **Psychological Distress:** Anxiety, despair, and emotional dysregulation are all examples of physical stress symptoms that can lead to psychological suffering. Chronic pain or discomfort might intensify sentiments of hopelessness, frustration, or despair.
- **Impaired Functioning:** Chronic stress and its physical manifestations can impair cognitive functioning, attention, memory, and decision-making skills, jeopardizing academic, occupational, and social functioning.

## Coping Strategies for Physical Signs of Stress

When faced with physical signs of stress, developing appropriate coping skills is critical for controlling our reactions and boosting resilience. While there is no one-size-fits-all answer, the following tactics may assist individuals in dealing with the issues of physical stress symptoms:

- **Stress Management Techniques:** Deep breathing exercises, gradual muscle relaxation, and mindfulness meditation are all stress management practices that can help you relax and reduce your physiological arousal levels.
- **Physical Activity:** Regular physical activity can help relieve muscle tension, enhance circulation, and stimulate the release of endorphins, which are natural mood-boosting substances that counteract stress. Choose activities that you enjoy and work them into your everyday routine.
- **Healthy Lifestyle Habits:** Put self-care activities that nourish your body, mind, and spirit first, such as balanced nutrition, enough sleep, hydration, and relaxation techniques. Avoid consuming too much caffeine, alcohol, or tobacco, as these might increase stress symptoms.
- **Social Support:** Seek social help from friends, family, or support groups who can offer understanding, validation, and practical assistance in dealing with physical stress symptoms. Make connections and cultivate relationships that provide a sense of belonging and support.
- **Professional treatment:** If physical stress symptoms are interfering with your quality of life or functioning, do not hesitate to seek professional treatment. A healthcare practitioner, therapist, or other mental health professional can offer support, guidance, and evidence-based therapies to help you cope with physical stress symptoms while also promoting healing and recovery.

## Emotional Symptoms

Emotional symptoms of stress include a wide range of sensations, moods, and psychological experiences that emerge in reaction to life's demands and stresses. These symptoms can take many forms, ranging from brief bouts of annoyance or worry to more permanent sensations of overwhelm despair, or emotional numbness. While the particular emotional symptoms experienced might differ from person to person, some common manifestations of stress include:

**1. Anxiety:** Stress can cause anxiety, fear, or concern about prospective threats or uncertainties. Physical symptoms may include a rapid heartbeat, sweating, trembling, or shortness of breath, as well as cognitive signs such as racing thoughts, rumination, or catastrophic thinking.

**2. Depression:** Chronic or overwhelming stress can exacerbate the feelings of sadness, hopelessness, or despair that define depression. Individuals may notice hunger changes, sleep difficulties, weariness, or a loss of interest in previously favored activities.

**3. Irritability:** Stress can cause people to become more irritable, frustrated, or angry in response to minor setbacks. They may get quickly upset, impatient, or reactive in their interactions with others, resulting in disagreements or strained relationships.

**4. Mood Swings:** Stress levels can fluctuate, causing individuals to experience fast shifts between highs and lows in their mood or affect. These mood swings may be associated with feelings of emotional instability or unpredictability.

**5. Emotional Numbness:** Chronic stress can cause emotional numbness or detachment, in which people feel disconnected from their feelings or have a diminished sense of pleasure or happiness. This emotional numbness may be used as a coping method to defend against intense emotions of anguish or vulnerability.

**6. Cognitive Distortions:** Stress can alter our perceptions of reality, resulting in erroneous beliefs about oneself, others, and the world. Individuals may participate in black-and-white thinking, magnifying unpleasant events, or personalizing blame, which exacerbates stress and misery.

## Impacts of Emotional Symptoms of Stress

The emotional symptoms of stress not only impair our subjective sense of well-being, but they can also have serious consequences for our mental health, relationships, and general quality of life. Chronic stress and its associated emotional symptoms, if not addressed, can contribute to a wide range of psychological issues and exacerbate pre-existing mental health conditions. Some common consequences of emotional signs of stress include:

- **Mental Health Disorders:** Prolonged stress and accompanying emotional symptoms might raise the likelihood of developing anxiety disorders, mood disorders (e.g., depression), post-traumatic stress disorder (PTSD), or adjustment problems. Stress-related emotional symptoms can exacerbate pre-existing mental health disorders or cause relapses during rehabilitation.
- **Relationship Strain:** Emotional stress symptoms can strain interpersonal relationships, resulting in disagreements, misunderstandings, and communication breakdowns. Individuals may withdraw socially or become emotionally unavailable to their loved ones, worsening feelings of isolation or loneliness.
- **Work Performance:** Stress-related emotional symptoms can decrease cognitive function, focus, and decision-making abilities, affecting academic, occupational, and social well-being. Individuals may struggle to meet deadlines, handle obligations, and perform well in their professional or academic endeavors.
- **Quality of Life:** Chronic stress and associated emotional symptoms can hurt one's entire quality of life, reducing feelings of contentment, fulfillment, and well-being. Individuals may experience a loss of purpose, meaning, or joy in their daily activities, resulting in feelings of despair or resignation.

# Coping Strategies for Emotional Symptoms of Stress

When confronted with emotional symptoms of stress, developing good coping techniques is critical for managing our reactions and boosting resilience. While no one-size-fits-all solution exists, the following tactics may assist individuals in navigating the problems of emotional symptoms of stress:

- **Emotion Regulation Techniques:** Use mindfulness meditation, deep breathing exercises, or progressive muscle relaxation to increase emotional awareness and establish healthy stress-coping strategies.
- **Cognitive Restructuring:** Challenge negative thought patterns and cognitive distortions by framing stressful situations in a more balanced and helpful manner. Develop self-compassion and a mindset of resilience, optimism, and self-efficacy.
- **Expressive Writing:** Journaling or expressive writing can be a safe place to manage emotions, gain insight into stress triggers, and explore new perspectives. Write freely and openly about your thoughts, feelings, and experiences, with no judgment or censoring.
- **Seek Social Support:** Contact friends, family members, or support groups for empathy, validation, and practical help dealing with emotional stress symptoms. Make connections and cultivate relationships that provide a sense of belonging and support.
- **Professional treatment:** If emotional stress symptoms are interfering with your quality of life and functioning, do not hesitate to seek professional treatment. A therapist, , m..counselor, or mental health professional can offer support, guidance, and evidence-based therapies to help you cope with stress-related emotional symptoms while also promoting healing and recovery.

# Behavioral Symptoms

Behavioral signs of stress include a wide range of observable acts, habits, and responses that reveal how stress affects our thoughts, feelings, and behaviors. These symptoms can take many forms, ranging from mild changes in behavior to more severe disturbances in daily functioning. While the particular behavioral symptoms observed can differ from person to person, some common expressions of stress include:

1. **Changes in Eating Habits:** Stress can affect our eating habits, causing changes in appetite, food preferences, and eating patterns. Some people may develop an increased appetite and cravings for comfort foods high in sugar, fat, or carbohydrates, whilst others may lose their appetite or participate in emotional eating as a coping mechanism.

2. **Sleep Disturbances:** Stress can disturb sleep habits, making it harder to get asleep, stay asleep, or get enough restorative sleep. Individuals may have insomnia, frequent awakenings, or nightmares as a result of heightened arousal and hyperarousal states caused by stress.

3. **Substance Abuse:** Stress can raise the risk of substance abuse or dependency because people use alcohol, drugs, or other substances to cope with stress or escape overwhelming feelings. Substance misuse can worsen stress symptoms, resulting in addiction, poor functioning, and negative health outcomes.

4. **Procrastination or Avoidance:** Stress can cause individuals to delay or avoid jobs or responsibilities that they see as burdensome or overwhelming. Procrastination may bring a brief reprieve from stress, but it might eventually lead to increasing feelings of anxiety, guilt, or self-criticism.

5. **Social Withdrawal:** Individuals who are stressed are more likely to withdraw or isolate themselves from social interactions and activities that they once enjoyed. Social withdrawal may be used as a coping method to conserve energy

and avoid potential stresses or triggers.

**6. Aggression or Irritability:** Stress can increase the chance of violent or irritable behavior as people struggle to cope with frustration, rage, or resentment. They may lash out verbally or violently at others, or engage in confrontational behavior in response to perceived threats or provocations.

## The effects of stress-related behavioural symptoms

Stress-related behavioural symptoms have a wide-ranging impact on our relationships, work performance, and overall quality of life. Chronic stress and its related behavioral manifestations, if not addressed, can lead to a variety of social, occupational, and health issues. Some common effects of behavioral indicators of stress include:

- **Interpersonal Conflict:** Stress-related behaviors can affect interpersonal relationships, resulting in disagreements, misunderstandings, or communication breakdowns. Individuals may struggle to properly express their needs or emotions, resulting in feelings of resentment, alienation, or separation.
- **Work Performance:** Stress-related behavioural symptoms can impair cognitive function, concentration, and decision-making skills, affecting academic, occupational, and social functioning. Individuals may struggle to meet deadlines, handle obligations, and perform well in their professional or academic endeavors.
- **Health Problems:** Chronic stress and related behavioural symptoms can contribute to a wide range of health issues, including cardiovascular disease, gastrointestinal disorders, immunological malfunction, and mental health disorders like anxiety and depression. Unhealthy behaviors, such as substance misuse or poor food, can worsen stress symptoms and contribute to the development or progression of chronic diseases.
- **Quality of Life:** Stress-related behavioural symptoms can reduce the overall quality of life by undermining emotions of contentment, fulfill-

ment, and well-being. Individuals may lose a sense of purpose, meaning, or joy in their daily activities, which can lead to sentiments of despair, resignation, or hopelessness.

## Coping Strategies for Stress-Related Symptoms

When dealing with stress-related behavioural symptoms, it is critical to developing effective coping techniques for controlling our reactions and boosting resilience. While no one-size-fits-all solution exists, the following tactics may assist individuals in navigating the obstacles of stress-related behavioral symptoms:

- **Stress Management Techniques:** Deep breathing exercises, gradual muscle relaxation, and mindfulness meditation are all stress management practices that can help you relax and reduce your physiological arousal levels.
- **Healthy Coping Mechanisms:** Identify and implement healthy coping strategies to replace maladaptive behaviors including substance addiction, procrastination, and social withdrawal. Seek out other stress-management strategies, such as exercise, artistic expression, or spending time in nature.
- **Time Management:** Improve your time management abilities by prioritizing chores, setting realistic goals, and making time for yourself. To avoid feeling overwhelmed, break down work into smaller, more manageable chunks and delegate responsibility as needed.
- **Social Support:** Seek social help from friends, family, or support groups who can offer understanding, validation, and practical assistance in dealing with stress-related behavioural problems. Make connections and cultivate relationships that provide a sense of belonging and support.
- **Professional treatment:** If stress-related behavioural symptoms are interfering with your quality of life or functioning, do not hesitate to seek professional treatment. A therapist, counselor, or mental health professional can offer support, guidance, and evidence-based therapies

to help you cope with stress-related behavioural symptoms while also promoting healing and recovery.

4

# CHAPTER THREE: CAUSES OF STRESS

## Biological Factors

I n the complicated web of human existence, stress is shaped not only by external circumstances and internal perspectives but also by a complex interaction of biological elements that influence our physiological reactions to life's difficulties. From the complicated circuitry of our neurological system to the delicate balance of hormones coursing through our bodies, biological variables have a significant impact on how we perceive, experience, and deal with stress.

## Understanding Biological Factors & Stress

Biological variables include a wide range of physiological mechanisms and processes that influence our bodies' responses to stimuli. These elements work on various levels, ranging from the cellular and molecular to the organ systems and neurological circuits that control our stress reactions. Some important biological elements that influence our stress responses include:

**1. The Nervous System:** Both the central nervous system (CNS) and the peripheral nervous system (PNS) play important roles in how we respond to stress. The hypothalamic-pituitary-adrenal (HPA) axis is a fundamental neuroendocrine system that regulates stress reactions. The sympathetic nervous system (SNS) activates the body's fight-or-flight reaction in the face of perceived dangers, whereas the parasympathetic nervous system (PNS) promotes balance and relaxation.

**2. Neurotransmitters:** Neurotransmitters are chemical messengers that carry signals from neurons in the brain and nervous system. Norepinephrine, dopamine, serotonin, and gamma-aminobutyric acid (GABA) are major neurotransmitters involved in stress responses. Imbalanced neurotransmitter levels can affect mood, arousal, and emotional control, contributing to stress-related disorders like anxiety and depression.

**3. Hormones:** Hormones are signaling molecules produced by the body's glands and organs, such as the adrenal glands, thyroid gland, and reproductive organs. Cortisol, adrenaline, and noradrenaline are key stress hormones that mobilize energy resources, regulate metabolism, and modulate immunological function. Hormonal dysregulation can impair the body's ability to respond to stress and maintain homeostasis.

**4. Genetics:** Genetic variables influence individual sensitivity to stress and stress-related diseases. Variations in genes that encode stress-related neurotransmitter receptors, hormone receptors, or enzymes involved in stress hormone metabolism can increase a person's chance of developing anxiety disorders, mood disorders, or post-traumatic stress disorder (PTSD).

**5. Epigenetics:** Epigenetic systems control gene expression and cellular function in response to environmental stimuli, including stress. Environmental factors such as early-life experiences, food, exercise, and exposure to chemicals or pollutants can alter epigenetic markers and influence the expression of stress-related genes. Epigenetic changes may contribute to the onset or persistence of stress-related diseases throughout the lifetime.

# Effects of Biological Factors on Stress

The interaction of biological components has a significant impact on how we perceive, experience, and respond to stress, influencing our physiological and psychological well-being in deep ways. Dysregulation of biological processes can cause a variety of health issues and raise the likelihood of acquiring stress-related diseases. Some common effects of biological factors on stress are:

- **Physical Health Problems:** Dysregulation of stress-related biological systems can lead to a wide range of physical health issues, including cardiovascular disease, gastrointestinal disorders, immunological dysfunction, metabolic disorders, and chronic pain syndromes. Prolonged activation of the stress response can worsen inflammation, impair immunological function, and contribute to the development or progression of chronic illnesses.
- **Mental Health Disorders:** Dysregulation of neurotransmitter systems, hormone systems, or hereditary factors can all raise the chance of developing mental health problems such as anxiety, mood, and psychotic illnesses. Imbalances in neurotransmitter levels or abnormalities in brain circuitry involved in stress responses can all lead to symptoms including anxiety, depression, and psychosis.
- **Behavioral Symptoms:** Dysregulation of biological variables can appear as hunger fluctuations, sleep difficulties, substance misuse, or mood swings. These behavioral manifestations may be coping methods or maladaptive responses to stresses, aggravating the stress-dysfunction cycle.
- **Cognitive impairments:** Dysregulation of stress-related biological systems can affect cognitive function, attention, memory, and decision-making skills. Chronic stress and its impact on neurotransmitter levels, as well as brain structure and function, may contribute to cognitive deficiencies including difficulty concentrating, learning, or problem-solving.
- **Interpersonal interactions:** Dysregulation of stress-related biological systems can interfere with interpersonal interactions, resulting in con-

flicts, misunderstandings, or communication breakdowns. Individuals may struggle to regulate their emotions and respond appropriately to social cues, resulting in strained relationships or social disengagement.

## Environmental Factors

Environmental factors include a wide range of external stimuli, situations, and contexts that might influence how people perceive stress. These elements can vary greatly in nature and extent, affecting both the physical and social aspects of the environment. Some important environmental elements that lead to stress are:

**1. Physical Environment:** Noise levels, air quality, temperature, and congestion can all have an impact on our stress levels. High levels of noise pollution, air pollution, or severe temperatures can all cause discomfort, irritability, and anxiety. In contrast, exposure to natural areas such as parks, woods, or bodies of water helps soothe the nervous system and encourage relaxation.

**2. Social surroundings:** The social dynamics and interactions in our surroundings can have a significant impact on our stress responses. Social support networks, ties with family, friends, and colleagues, as well as the quality of interpersonal interactions, can all have an impact on our sense of belonging, security, and well-being. Conflict, rejection, and social isolation are all examples of social stresses that can exacerbate feelings of loneliness, alienation, and misery.

**3. Work Environment:** The organizational culture, work expectations, and job-related stressors in the workplace can all have an impact on our stress levels and overall health. workplace instability, a heavy workload, a lack of control or autonomy, bad interpersonal relationships, and role ambiguity can all lead to feelings of workplace stress, burnout, or discontent.

**4. Community Environment:** The qualities of the community in which we live, such as socioeconomic status, resource availability, neighborhood safety, and social cohesiveness, can all have an impact on our stress and health outcomes. Disparities in healthcare, education, work, and housing can intensify emotions of inequity, injustice, or powerlessness, resulting in chronic stress and poor health consequences.

**5. Cultural Environment:** Cultural norms, values, and beliefs influence our perceptions of stress and how we deal with adversity. Cultural issues such as mental health stigma, gender roles, attitudes toward work-life balance, and stress management rituals or practices can all have an impact on how we respond to stress and whether we seek help or support.

## The effects of environmental factors on stress

Environmental stressors can have a wide-ranging impact on our physical health, mental well-being, and overall quality of life. Environmental stressors can increase pre-existing vulnerabilities, contributing to a wide range of health issues and socioeconomic inequities. Some common effects of environmental influences on stress are:

- **Physical Health Problems:** Environmental stressors such as air pollution, noise pollution, and urban crowding can cause several physical health issues, including cardiovascular disease, respiratory ailments, gastrointestinal disorders, and immunological dysfunction. Chronic exposure to environmental chemicals or pollutants can worsen inflammation, impair immunological function, and raise the risk of chronic illnesses.

- **Mental Health Disorders:** Environmental stressors such as social isolation, neighborhood violence, or professional stress can all contribute to the development or worsening of mental health disorders such as anxiety disorders, mood disorders, and post-traumatic stress disorder (PTSD). Chronic exposure to social stresses or traumatic life experiences might damage the brain circuitry involved in stress responses, increasing the chance of developing mental symptoms.

- **Workplace Burnout:** Organisational culture, work expectations, and job-related pressures can all contribute to feelings of burnout, discontent, and turnover. High levels of job-related stress can impair cognitive function, focus, and decision-making skills, resulting in lower productivity, absenteeism, and higher healthcare expenses for businesses.
- **Social Disparities:** Environmental factors such as socioeconomic level, resource availability, and neighborhood characteristics can all contribute to differences in stress exposure and health outcomes. Individuals in low-income or marginalized groups may be exposed to disproportionately high levels of environmental stressors, such as insufficient housing, food insecurity, violence, and limited access to healthcare and social services.
- **Quality of Life:** Environmental stresses can reduce overall quality of life by eroding perceptions of safety, security, and well-being. Chronic exposure to environmental stressors can cause feelings of helplessness, hopelessness, or despair, resulting in lower life satisfaction and resilience in the face of adversity.

## Psychological Factors

Psychological factors include a wide range of internal processes, beliefs, attitudes, and coping techniques that shape how we perceive, interpret, and respond to stressors. These elements interact with our thoughts, emotions, and behaviors, influencing our subjective experience of stress as well as our ability to adapt and prosper in the face of adversity. Some important psychological aspects that contribute to our experiences with stress include:

**1. Cognitive Appraisals:** Cognitive appraisals describe how we perceive and interpret stressful circumstances. Our evaluations can impact whether we perceive a situation as scary, difficult, or controllable, and they can shape our emotional and behavioral responses appropriately. Positive assessments that emphasize our abilities to cope with stressors might boost resilience, whereas negative appraisals that emphasize helplessness or catastrophizing can worsen discomfort.

**2. Beliefs and Attitudes:** Our beliefs and attitudes regarding stress, adversity, and our ability to deal with difficulties might influence how we react to stressful events. Individuals who believe "I can handle whatever comes my way" or "I grow stronger through adversity" are more likely to confront challenges with hope, self-efficacy, and resilience. Individuals who believe that "I'm helpless in the face of stress" or "I'll never be able to cope" may experience increased anxiety, hopelessness, or despair.

**3. Coping Strategies:** Coping strategies are the actions and behaviors that we use to manage the demands of stressful situations. Adaptive coping strategies, such as problem-solving, seeking social support, and practicing relaxation techniques, can help reduce stress and improve emotional well-being. Avoidance, denial, and substance misuse are examples of maladaptive coping mechanisms that may provide brief respite but can eventually increase pain and damage long-term resilience.

**4. Emotional Regulation:** Emotional regulation is the ability to modify and govern our emotions in response to stimuli. Effective emotional regulation skills enable us to tolerate distress, manage arousal, and maintain balance in the face of adversity. People with excellent emotional regulation abilities are better able to deal with stress, resolve problems, and maintain healthy relationships.

**5. Resilience:** Resilience is the ability to recover from adversity, adapt to change, and prosper in the face of obstacles. Resilient people have a combination of psychological traits including self-awareness, optimism, flexibility, and social support that allow them to weather life's storms with grace and resilience. Resilience is not a set attribute, but rather a dynamic process that may be developed and reinforced over time through self-reflection, coping skills, and social connections.

## Effects of Psychological Factors on Stress

The interaction of psychological elements has a significant impact on how we perceive, experience, and respond to stress, influencing our psychological and emotional well-being in deep ways. Positive psychological characteristics including optimism, self-efficacy, and adaptive coping mechanisms can help us build resilience and cope with challenges. In contrast, negative psychological characteristics such as pessimism learned helplessness, and maladaptive coping techniques can worsen suffering and contribute to the development or exacerbation of stress-related diseases. Some common effects of psychological factors on stress are:

- **Emotional Well-being:** Cognitive assessments, beliefs, and attitudes can all have a significant impact on our emotional well-being and resilience to stress. People who handle challenges with optimism, self-efficacy, and adaptive coping techniques are more likely to have positive feelings, higher life satisfaction, and lower levels of psychological discomfort.
- **Mental Health Disorders:** Negative psychological factors such as rumination, catastrophizing, or emotional avoidance can contribute to the development or worsening of mental health problems such as anxiety disorders, mood disorders, and post-traumatic stress disorder (PTSD). Maladaptive coping mechanisms, such as substance misuse or self-harm, may provide short-term respite but eventually contribute to the cycle of pain and dysfunction.
- **Physical Health:** Physical health outcomes can be influenced by psychological variables such as chronic stress or negative emotions, which disrupt physiological processes such as immunological function, cardiovascular function, and inflammatory responses. Chronic activation of the stress response can raise the chance of acquiring chronic diseases like hypertension, diabetes, and autoimmune disorders.
- **Social Relationships:** Interpersonal skills, emotional control, and resilience are all psychological traits that can have an impact on the quality of our social relationships and support systems. Individuals with strong

social support networks and great communication skills are better able to negotiate problems, seek help, and support others in need.

- **Quality of Life:** Psychological elements influence our feeling of purpose, meaning, and fulfillment in life. Positive psychological variables such as thankfulness, self-compassion, and resilience can help us find purpose and joy in life's obstacles, but negative psychological elements like pessimism, rumination, or emotional avoidance can reduce our sense of well-being and contentment.

## Coping Strategies for Psychological Factors and Stress.

While psychological factors might influence our stress responses, some activities can be performed to build positive psychological qualities and promote resilience in the face of adversity. These tactics could include:

- **Cognitive Restructuring:** Challenge negative thought patterns and cognitive distortions by framing stressful situations in a more balanced and helpful manner. Use cognitive restructuring approaches like cognitive-behavioral therapy (CBT) to detect and confront illogical ideas, catastrophic thinking, and all-or-nothing thinking patterns.
- **Mindfulness and Meditation:** Practice mindfulness and meditation to increase awareness of your thoughts, emotions, and physiological sensations in the present. Mindfulness-based interventions can help reduce rumination, improve emotional regulation, and boost resilience in the face of stress.
- **Self-Compassion and Self-Care:** When dealing with stress, treat oneself with kindness, understanding, and acceptance. Be aware of your own needs and limitations, and prioritize activities that nourish your body, mind, and spirit.
- **Professional Help:** If psychological concerns are interfering with your quality of life or functioning, do not be afraid to seek professional help. A therapist, counsellor, or mental health professional can give support, guidance, and evidence-based therapies to help you cope with

psychological problems while promoting healing and resilience.

5

# CHAPTER FOUR: COPING STRATEGIES

## Relaxation Technique

Finding moments of tranquillity and quiet can feel like a rare luxury in today's fast-paced world. However, amid the stress and pressures of daily life, cultivating relaxation becomes not only a luxury but also a requirement for preserving our physical, mental, and emotional well-being. Relaxation techniques provide a haven amidst the storm, giving us tools to unwind, recharge, and restore equilibrium to our bodies and brains.

## Understanding Relaxation Techniques

Relaxation techniques include a wide range of practices and procedures that aim to increase relaxation while reducing physiological and psychological arousal. These techniques use ideas from mindfulness, meditation, breath-work, progressive muscle relaxation, and guided imagery to help people release stress, quiet their minds, and build a sense of peace and well-being. Relaxation techniques, whether used singly or in combination, provide a comprehensive approach to stress alleviation that targets both the mind and the body. Some frequent relaxing techniques are:

**1. Deep Breathing:** Deep breathing exercises are deliberate and conscious breathing patterns that slow down the breath, trigger the body's relaxation response, and create sensations of peace and relaxation. Techniques including diaphragmatic breathing, square breathing, and counting breaths can assist in controlling the autonomic nervous system, lower stress hormones, and induce relaxation.

**2. Progressive Muscle Relaxation (PMR):** Progressive Muscle Relaxation (PMR) is the process of systematically tensing and releasing various muscle groups in the body to relieve physical stress and promote relaxation. Individuals can increase their awareness of muscle tension and learn to release it consciously by alternating between tensing and relaxing muscles, resulting in a profound sense of relaxation and tranquillity.

**3. Mindfulness Meditation:** Mindfulness meditation is the practice of cultivating present-moment awareness and accepting one's thoughts, emotions, and bodily sensations without judgment. Mindfulness activities such as focused attention, body scan, and loving-kindness meditation can help people develop better clarity, equanimity, and resilience in the face of stressors, generating a sense of inner peace and well-being.

**4. Guided Imagery:** These approaches use visualization and imagination to elicit pleasant and relaxing mental images or scenarios. Individuals can reduce tension and promote relaxation by visualizing pleasant scenes such as a serene beach or tranquil woodland.

**5. Yoga and Tai Chi:** Yoga and Tai Chi are both ancient mind-body practices that use physical postures, breathwork, and mindfulness techniques to improve relaxation, flexibility, and balance. These practices promote inner harmony, calm, and well-being through gentle movement, breath awareness, and meditation.

## Benefits of Relaxation Techniques

The use of relaxation techniques has numerous benefits for our physical, mental, and emotional health. These strategies, which promote relaxation and reduce stress, can improve our general quality of life and resilience in the face of life's obstacles. Some major advantages of relaxation techniques include:

- **tension Reduction:** Relaxation techniques are extremely effective at reducing tension and increasing relaxation. These techniques activate the body's relaxation response, lowering stress chemicals like cortisol and adrenaline, reducing muscle tension, and quieting the mind, resulting in a deep sensation of serenity and well-being.
- **Improved Sleep:** Relaxation practices can assist improve sleep quality and reduce insomnia by encouraging relaxation and lowering alertness before to bedtime. Deep breathing, gradual muscle relaxation, and guided imagery can all help people relax, clear their minds, and prepare for a good night's sleep.
- **Enhanced Mental Clarity:** Regular relaxation exercises can help to sharpen mental focus, improve cognitive function, and increase concentration and productivity. By eliminating mental clutter and encouraging mindfulness, these strategies assist individuals in developing clarity, creativity, and resilience in the face of mental problems.
- **Emotional Regulation:** Relaxation techniques are effective strategies for controlling emotions and increasing emotional resilience. Individuals who practice present-moment awareness and self-compassion can learn to negotiate challenging emotions like anxiety, rage, or grief with greater ease and equanimity, promoting emotional well-being and balance.
- **Physical Health Benefits:** Relaxation techniques have been linked to a variety of physical health benefits, including lower blood pressure, improved cardiovascular function, increased immune function, and a lower risk of chronic diseases such as heart disease, diabetes, and autoimmune disorders. These approaches promote relaxation and reduce

the physiological impacts of stress, resulting in improved health and vitality.

## Integrating Relaxation Techniques into Everyday Life

Integrating relaxation techniques into our regular routines can help us relieve stress and achieve inner peace. Setting aside time for relaxation and self-care allows us to create moments of respite from the stresses of daily life, developing a sense of balance, resilience, and well-being. Here are some practical strategies for implementing relaxation techniques into your daily life:

- **Create a Relaxation Ritual:** Set up a regular relaxation ritual that you can incorporate into your daily routine, such as deep breathing exercises before bedtime, a thoughtful walk during your lunch break, or a few minutes of meditation or guided imagery each morning.
- **Set boundaries:** Prioritise self-care by limiting your time, energy, and obligations. Learn to say no to activities or obligations that deplete your resources and leave you feeling stressed, and set aside time for relaxation and self-care.
- **Practice Gratitude:** Develop a grateful mindset by meditating on your life's benefits and joys. Spend a few moments each day acknowledging and appreciating the small joys, moments of beauty, and acts of generosity that bring light into your life, promoting contentment and well-being.
- **Engage in Mindful Activities:** Incorporate mindfulness into your everyday routine by bringing awareness and presence to whatever you're doing, whether it's eating, showering, or doing the dishes. By practicing mindfulness in everyday situations, you can build a sense of serenity and centering amid life's chaos.
- **Seek Support:** Seek help from friends, family members, or support groups who can offer empathy, encouragement, and accountability as you embark on your relaxing journey. Share your experiences, problems, and accomplishments with others, and be inspired by their stories and

thoughts.

## Mindfulness and Meditation

Mindfulness and meditation are two closely linked techniques that emphasize present-moment awareness, nonjudgmental acceptance, and loving presence. While the terms are frequently used interchangeably, mindfulness refers to the state of being completely engaged and aware of the present moment, whereas meditation refers to the deliberate practice of growing awareness through various techniques and exercises. Together, these activities provide a road to increased clarity, insight, and peace of mind.

Mindfulness meditation usually entails sitting silently and noticing the breath, body sensations, thoughts, and emotions as they arise in the present moment. By paying attentive attention to the sensations of the breath going in and out of the body, practitioners learn to focus their attention on the present now and build a sense of serenity and clarity amid mental fluctuations.

There are numerous types of meditation, each with its practices and goals. Some common forms of meditation include:

**1. Focused Attention Meditation:** In this technique, practitioners concentrate their attention on a single item or point of concentration, such as their breath, a mantra, or a visual image. By focusing their attention on a precise location, practitioners develop mental clarity, concentration, and relaxation.

**2. Loving-Kindness Meditation:** Loving-Kindness Meditation is a practice that involves growing feelings of love, compassion, and goodwill for oneself and others. Practitioners frequently repeat statements like "May I be happy, may I be healthy, may I be safe, may I live with ease," extending their wishes to themselves, loved ones, neutral folks, and even problematic people.

**3. Body Scan Meditation:** In this practice, practitioners scan their bodies from head to toe, paying attention to each portion and noting any sensations, tensions, or places of discomfort. Practitioners gain deeper awareness, relaxation, and embodiment by listening to their bodies with curiosity and compassion.

**4. Open Awareness Meditation:** Open Awareness Meditation entails remaining in open awareness, allowing ideas, emotions, and sensations to arise and pass without judgment or attachment. Practitioners examine the flow of experience with openness and acceptance, building a sense of calm and presence.

## Benefits of Mindfulness and Meditation

Mindfulness and meditation have numerous benefits to our physical, mental, and emotional well-being. These techniques have been proven to have a positive impact on all aspects of our lives, from stress and anxiety reduction to increased attention and resilience. Mindfulness and meditation have several major benefits, including:

- **Stress Reduction:** Mindfulness and meditation are effective methods for stress reduction and relaxation. By fostering present-moment mindfulness and compassionate acceptance, these activities assist individuals in breaking away from the cycle of rumination and concern, lowering physiological arousal and creating a sense of peace and well-being.
- **Improved Mental Health:** Mindfulness and meditation have been linked to lower levels of anxiety, depression, and other mental health conditions. These activities promote self-awareness, emotional regulation, and compassion, allowing individuals to traverse unpleasant emotions with more ease and resilience.
- **Enhanced Focus and Concentration:** Mindfulness and meditation are powerful strategies for improving cognitive function, attention, and concentration. These practices assist people create mental clarity, attentiveness, and efficiency in their daily activities by teaching them to stay focused on the present moment.
- **Greater Emotional Resilience:** Mindfulness and meditation practice

help people build a greater ability to tolerate and handle painful emotions. These practices encourage nonjudgmental acceptance and self-compassion, allowing people to respond to situations with greater equanimity and grace.

- **Improved Relationships:** Mindfulness and meditation increase empathy, compassion, and emotional regulation, which can improve the quality of our interactions with others. These techniques promote deeper relationships and understanding with others by fostering present-moment mindfulness and deep listening skills.

## Integrating Mindfulness and Meditation into Everyday Life

Integrating mindfulness and meditation into our daily routines can help us harness the transforming power of these practices, resulting in increased peace and well-being. Whether practiced officially in dedicated meditation sessions or informally throughout the day, mindfulness and meditation provide numerous opportunities to cultivate present and inner serenity. Here are some useful strategies for adopting mindfulness and meditation into your daily life:

- **Start small:** Set aside just a few minutes per day for mindfulness and meditation practice. Begin with brief 5- to 10-minute sessions and progressively increase the duration as you gain confidence in the exercise.
- **Find a Quiet area:** Designate an area for meditation where you may sit comfortably and without distractions. Choose a calm, serene setting where you may feel safe and relaxed, free of interruptions or external distractions.
- **Practice Regularly:** Consistency is essential in mindfulness and meditation practice. Aim to practice every day, even if only for a few minutes. Set out time in your schedule for meditation and consider it as a must-do component of your daily routine.
- **Be Patient and Gentle with Yourself:** Mindfulness and meditation are skills that require time and patience to acquire. Be kind to yourself, and

approach your practice with a sense of inquiry, openness, and compassion.

- **Integrate Mindfulness into Daily Activities:** Bring mindfulness into your daily activities by paying attention to the present moment as you go about your day. Practice mindful eating, walking, and driving by paying close attention to the sensations, sights, and sounds around you with curiosity and presence.

## Exercise and Physical Activity

Exercise and physical activity refer to a wide range of movement-based activities that include the body's muscles, bones, and cardiovascular system. There are numerous ways to include physical activity in our daily lives, including brisk walking and jogging, as well as swimming, cycling, yoga, and strength training. While exercise is frequently defined as a systematic and intentional movement intended to increase fitness and performance, physical activity refers to any type of body movement that expends energy and promotes health.

Regular physical activity is vital for preserving good health and well-being throughout life. The American Heart Association advises at least 150 minutes of moderate-intensity aerobic activity or 75 minutes of vigorous-intensity aerobic activity per week, as well as two or more days of muscle-strengthening activities. These guidelines provide a framework for improving cardiovascular health, maintaining a healthy weight, and lowering the risk of chronic diseases like heart disease, diabetes, and obesity.

## Benefits of Exercise and Physical Activity

Exercise and physical activity provide numerous benefits beyond physical fitness, including improved mental health, cognitive performance, emotional well-being, and social connectedness. Regular physical activity can lead to a variety of favorable effects that improve one's overall quality of life. Some important advantages of exercise and physical activity include:

- **Improved Cardiovascular Health:** Regular exercise strengthens the heart and circulation system, enhancing cardiovascular function and lowering the risk of heart attack, stroke, and hypertension. Aerobic exercises like walking, jogging, cycling, and swimming help to lower blood pressure, cholesterol, and triglycerides, which promotes heart health and longevity.

- **Improved Mood and Mental Health:** Exercise has been demonstrated to have potent antidepressant and anxiolytic properties, lowering symptoms of depression, anxiety, and stress. Physical activity causes the production of endorphins, which boost sensations of happiness, relaxation, and well-being, as well as an increase in serotonin and dopamine, which are neurotransmitters related to mood regulation and pleasure.

- **Cognitive Benefits:** Regular physical activity has been related to enhanced cognitive function, memory, and executive function. Exercise boosts blood flow to the brain, promotes the creation of new neurons, and improves neuroplasticity, or the brain's ability to change and reorganize in response to experience. These cognitive benefits lead to enhanced concentration, attention, and problem-solving abilities, as well as a lower risk of cognitive decline and dementia later in life.

- **Weight Management:** Exercise helps to manage weight by improving energy expenditure, lean muscle mass, and metabolism. Aerobic activities burn calories and promote fat reduction, whereas strength training increases muscle mass and metabolic rate, resulting in more efficient calorie burning at rest. A healthy weight can only be achieved and maintained via regular physical exercise and a well-balanced diet.

- **Enhanced Sleep Quality:** Exercise has been demonstrated to increase sleep quality and duration, allowing people to fall asleep faster, stay asleep longer, and have deeper, more restorative sleep. Physical activity modulates circadian rhythms, alleviates insomnia symptoms, and promotes relaxation, all of which contribute to improved sleep hygiene and overall happiness.

- **Increased Energy and Vitality:** Regular exercise increases energy and vitality by boosting circulation, oxygen delivery, and nutrient absorption throughout the body. Physical activity causes the release of adrenaline and other hormones, which boost alertness, focus, and energy levels, resulting in a stronger sense of vitality and vigor throughout the day.

- **Social Connection and Community:** Exercise promotes social connection and community participation, building friendships, camaraderie, and support groups. Group fitness classes, sports teams, and leisure activities provide opportunities for social connection and bonding, thereby alleviating feelings of loneliness, isolation, and depression.

## Integrating Exercise and Physical Activity into Everyday Life

Incorporating fitness and physical activity into our daily lives does not have to be difficult or time-consuming. By selecting things that we like and prioritizing movement, we can get the benefits of regular physical activity while also improving our overall quality of life. Here are some useful strategies for incorporating fitness and physical activity into your daily life:

- **Find things You Enjoy:** Select things that you truly enjoy and look forward to doing. Whether it's walking, dancing, hiking, swimming, or playing sports, discover things that bring you joy and fulfillment, making exercise feel less like a chore and more like a treat.
- **Set Realistic Goals:** Determine what you can achieve depending on your current fitness level, hobbies, and schedule. Begin with simple, realistic goals and progressively ramp up the intensity, duration, and frequency of your workouts as you develop. Celebrate your victories and be patient with yourself as you strive for your goals.
- **Make It a Habit:** Include regular exercise sessions in your daily or weekly schedule, seeing them as non-negotiable meetings with yourself. Set aside particular periods for physical activity and prioritize them just like you would any other significant commitment.
- **Mix It Up:** Keep your workouts interesting and entertaining by varying your regimen and attempting new activities. Include a variety of aerobic, strength training, flexibility, and balancing activities to keep your body challenged and your mind engaged.

- **Listen to your body:** Pay attention to your body's cues and tailor your workouts accordingly. If you're tired or uncomfortable, take a day off or participate in gentle, low-impact activities like yoga or stretching. Be aware of any pain or discomfort, and seek medical attention if necessary.
- **Stay Consistent:** Consistency is essential for getting the benefits of exercise and physical activity. Aim for frequent, consistent workouts rather than random, intensive periods of exertion. Remember that even modest quantities of exercise can have a major impact on your health and well-being over time.

6

# CHAPTER FIVE:
# COGNITIVE-BEHAVIORAL APPROACHES

## Cognitive Restructuring

In the complex geography of the human mind, our thoughts shape our perceptions, emotions, and behaviors in deep ways. However, all too frequently, our thoughts become distorted or skewed, sending us down roads of pessimism, self-doubt, and despair. Cognitive restructuring shines a light in the darkness, giving a strong framework for identifying, questioning, and transforming maladaptive thought patterns into those that promote resilience, optimism, and well-being.

## Understanding Cognitive Restructuring

Cognitive restructuring is a key technique drawn from cognitive-behavioral therapy (CBT), a well-studied and evidence-based approach to psychotherapy. Cognitive restructuring is essentially the process of detecting and confronting negative or distorted thought patterns known as cognitive distortions, and then replacing them with more balanced, accurate, and adaptable beliefs. Cognitive restructuring enables people to change their perceptions, reframe

47

their experiences, and nurture higher emotional well-being and resilience by addressing the underlying ideas and assumptions that drive maladaptive thinking.

The cognitive model of emotional reaction, which asserts that our thoughts, beliefs, and interpretations of events have a direct impact on our emotions and behaviors, serves as the foundation for cognitive restructuring. According to this paradigm, our emotional reactions are determined by the meaning we attribute to events through our thoughts and interpretations, rather than the events themselves. By modifying our thinking, we may change our emotional responses and, as a result, our worldviews.

## Common cognitive distortions

Recognizing and confronting cognitive distortions, or biassed or irrational thought processes that contribute to emotional pain and dysfunctional behavior, is central to cognitive restructuring therapy. Cognitive distortions can appear in a variety of contexts, including relationships, jobs, and self-perception. Some typical cognitive distortions are:

**1. All-or-Nothing Thinking:** This distortion involves viewing events as black-and-white, with no middle ground or shades of grey. People who believe in all-or-nothing thinking tend to regard things as either perfect or a complete disaster, leaving no opportunity for nuance or flexibility.

**2. Catastrophizing:** Catastrophizing entails exaggerating the significance or prospective implications of unfavorable events, anticipating the worst-case scenario, and believing that tragedy is unavoidable. This incorrect thinking pattern can cause increased anxiety, fear, and avoidance behaviors.

**3. Mind Reading:** Mind reading is the process of forming assumptions about what others are thinking or feeling without providing evidence to back them up. People who do mind reading frequently jump to conclusions and misread others' behavior, resulting in misunderstandings and confrontations.

**4. Discounting the Positive:** This distortion is ignoring or minimizing positive experiences, accomplishments, or attributes while focusing solely on the negative parts of an event. People who devalue the positive may fail to recognize their qualities and successes, leading to feelings of inadequacy or low self-esteem.

**5. Emotional Reasoning:** Emotional thinking is the assumption that our feelings reflect objective reality, without evaluating alternative explanations or evidence. People who use emotional reasoning may believe that if they feel something, it must be real, regardless of the facts or circumstances of the scenario.

**6. Overgeneralization:** Overgeneralization is the process of extrapolating broad generalizations from limited facts or isolated instances. People who overgeneralize may use terms like "always" or "never" to describe their experiences, creating an exaggerated sense of inevitability or permanence.

## Principles of Cognitive Restructuring

Cognitive restructuring entails numerous essential principles and approaches for confronting and reframing cognitive distortions. These concepts are based on the idea that human thoughts are not necessarily accurate or objective representations of reality, but rather subjective interpretations impacted by a range of circumstances such as prior experiences, beliefs, and cultural influences. Some key principles of cognitive reorganization are:

- **Identifying Cognitive Distortions:** The first stage in cognitive restructuring is to become aware of and recognize cognitive distortions as they appear in our thoughts. To recognize when we are involved in erroneous thought patterns, we must first cultivate mindfulness and self-awareness.
- **Challenging Negative Thoughts:** After identifying cognitive distortions, the next stage is to challenge and question their validity. This entails weighing the facts for and against the mistaken notion, evaluating

alternate interpretations, and developing more balanced and realistic viewpoints.

- **Generating Alternative Thoughts:** After confronting negative thoughts, the next stage is to generate alternative, more balanced thoughts based on evidence and reason. This could include rephrasing the situation in a more positive perspective, evaluating different explanations or points of view, and recognizing strengths and resources.
- **Testing Assumptions and Ideas:** Cognitive restructuring also entails challenging the underlying assumptions and ideas that fuel our negative thinking. This may entail obtaining data to support or disprove our views, weighing the consequences of maintaining those beliefs, and investigating more adaptive options.
- **Behavioral Experiments:** In some cases, cognitive restructuring may entail running behavioral experiments to verify the validity of our beliefs and assumptions in real-world scenarios. This could include experimenting with new behaviors, taking measured risks, and collecting data to assess the results of our efforts.

## Techniques for Cognitive restructuring

Cognitive restructuring refers to a variety of strategies and activities used to confront and reframe cognitive biases. These strategies can be used in a variety of settings, including individual therapy, self-help interventions, and everyday living. Some popular approaches for cognitive reorganization are:

- **Thought Records:** Thought diaries are structured workbooks for tracking and analyzing negative thoughts, feelings, and behaviors. Typically, thought records consist of recognizing the triggering event, recording the automatic ideas that arise in reaction to the event, challenging and reframing those thoughts, and assessing the influence of the reframed thoughts on emotions and behaviors.
- **Socratic Questioning:** Socratic questioning entails asking probing questions to challenge and investigate the validity of negative ideas and beliefs.

This strategy helps people to look at the evidence for and against their ideas, to consider different points of view, and to come up with more balanced explanations for events.

- **Mindfulness and Acceptance:** Meditation, deep breathing, and body scan exercises can all help you develop present-moment awareness and nonjudgmental acceptance of thoughts and feelings. Individuals can minimize the emotional impact of negative thoughts by observing them with curiosity and compassion.
- **Cognitive Restructuring Worksheets:** These worksheets offer systematic prompts and exercises for recognizing, questioning, and reframing cognitive distortions. These worksheets may include areas for documenting negative thoughts, creating alternative thoughts, and assessing the validity of beliefs.
- **Visualization and Imagery:** These approaches use mental imagery to question and reframe undesirable attitudes and beliefs. This could include imagining oneself successfully dealing with a difficult situation, visualizing a pleasant outcome, or picturing oneself overcoming hurdles and accomplishing goals.

## Applications for Cognitive Restructuring

Anxiety, sadness, stress, low self-esteem, and relationship problems are all examples of issues and obstacles that can be addressed with cognitive restructuring. Cognitive restructuring, whether employed in individual therapy, self-help initiatives, or everyday life, provides a powerful framework for boosting emotional resilience, improving problem-solving skills, and developing adaptive coping strategies.

In the context of anxiety disorders, cognitive restructuring can assist people in challenging illogical worries, catastrophic thinking, and avoidance behaviors, allowing them to address their anxieties and gradually expose themselves to anxiety-provoking events. Individuals who reframe negative attitudes and beliefs about themselves, others, and the world might gain better confidence, self-efficacy, and resilience in the face of worry.

In the therapy of depression, cognitive restructuring can assist individuals in challenging and rephrasing negative self-talk, self-critical ideas, and pessimistic future assumptions. Individuals who replace erroneous views with more balanced and accurate viewpoints can lessen feelings of hopelessness, worthlessness, and despair while increasing sentiments of hope, optimism, and self-worth.

In terms of stress management, cognitive restructuring can assist individuals in identifying and challenging negative attitudes and beliefs that contribute to feelings of overwhelm, burnout, and weariness. By adopting a more adaptive mentality and reframing difficult experiences as chances for growth and learning, individuals can cultivate better resilience, flexibility, and coping abilities in the face of life's obstacles.

## Stress Inoculation Training

Stress inoculation training is a psychotherapy strategy that tries to prepare people to cope with stress by exposing them to manageable amounts of stress in a safe and supportive setting. Stress inoculation training, which is based on cognitive-behavioral therapy (CBT) principles, provides individuals with a toolkit of coping strategies, relaxation techniques, and cognitive restructuring skills to help them navigate stressful situations more easily and resiliently.

The concept of stress inoculation is analogous to vaccination, in which exposure to a weakened or harmless form of a pathogen primes the immune system to generate a protective response against subsequent infections. Similarly, exposure to regulated levels of stress in a supportive and therapeutic setting can help people develop resilience and adaptive coping abilities that protect them from the detrimental consequences of stress in everyday life.

### The Principles of Stress Inoculation Training

Stress inoculation training is governed by several important principles and strategies designed to help people manage effectively with stress. These concepts are based on the idea that resilience is a talent that can be developed and reinforced via rigorous training and practice. Some important principles of stress inoculation training are:

- **Education and Psychoeducation:** The initial step of stress inoculation training entails teaching individuals about the nature of stress, its effects on the mind and body, and effective stress-management coping strategies. Psychoeducation enables people to get a better knowledge of the stress response, challenge common misconceptions about stress, and learn practical stress-management strategies.
- **Skill Building:** Stress inoculation training focuses on the development of specific coping skills and practices to assist people in better managing stress. These abilities may include relaxation techniques like deep breathing, progressive muscle relaxation, and guided imagery, as well as cognitive restructuring approaches to confront negative attitudes and beliefs that cause stress.
- **Stress Exposure and Desensitisation:** Stress inoculation training relies heavily on gradual exposure to stressors in a controlled and supportive environment. This exposure allows people to develop stress tolerance and adaptive coping strategies that will help them handle stress more efficiently in the long run. Individuals learn to address their concerns, regulate their emotions, and problem-solve more successfully in stressful situations as they are exposed to stressors repeatedly.
- **Cognitive Restructuring:** Stress inoculation training uses cognitive restructuring strategies to help people challenge and reframe negative attitudes and beliefs that cause stress and anxiety. Individuals can improve their coping abilities by identifying and confronting unreasonable or distorted thought processes.
- **Role Playing and Rehearsal:** Stress inoculation training frequently includes role-playing and rehearsal of stressful circumstances to allow participants to practice coping strategies in a simulated setting. Role-playing allows people to experiment with different stress-management tactics while receiving feedback and support from therapists or peers.
- **Social Support and Coping Resources:** Stress inoculation training em-

phasizes the role of social support and coping resources in mitigating the detrimental effects of stress. Individuals can improve their resilience and coping skills in the face of hardship by connecting with people, seeking assistance from friends, family members, or support groups, and utilizing community resources.

## Techniques for Stress Inoculation Training

Stress inoculation training includes several approaches and activities aimed at increasing resilience, improving coping abilities, and mitigating the effects of stress on mental and emotional well-being. These strategies can be adjusted to the unique needs and interests of participants. They may include:

- **Relaxation Training:** Relaxation training involves teaching individuals relaxation techniques such as deep breathing, progressive muscle relaxation, and guided imagery to help reduce physiological arousal and promote a sense of calm and well-being. These techniques can be practiced regularly as a preventive measure or used as coping strategies in response to acute stressors.
- **Cognitive Restructuring Exercises:** These exercises entail identifying and addressing negative thoughts and beliefs that lead to stress and anxiety. Participants learn to identify cognitive distortions like catastrophizing, overgeneralization, and black-and-white thinking, and then replace them with more balanced and adaptive views.
- **Stress Exposure and Desensitization:** Stress exposure and desensitization exercises include gradually exposing people to increasingly difficult or anxiety-inducing situations in a safe and supportive atmosphere. Therapists can help people build resilience and confidence in their capacity to deal with stress by progressively exposing them to stressors and assisting them in developing coping techniques to manage their emotions.
- **Problem-Solving Skills Training:** Problem-solving skills training offers people methodical methods for detecting, analyzing, and solving difficulties in their lives. Participants learn how to break down challenges into

manageable steps, develop alternate solutions, and assess the efficacy of various tactics.

· **Assertiveness Training:** Assertiveness training helps people build communication skills and assertive behaviors so they can effectively express their needs, preferences, and boundaries. Participants learn to assert themselves respectfully and confidently, which reduces interpersonal conflict and boosts their sense of self-efficacy and empowerment.

· **Social Support Enhancement:** Social support enhancement entails locating and utilizing sources of social support and coping resources in people's lives. Participants learn how to seek and maintain helpful relationships with friends, family, and support groups.

## Applications for Stress Inoculation Training

Anxiety disorders, depression, post-traumatic stress disorder (PTSD), chronic pain, and relationship problems are all examples of concerns and obstacles that can benefit from stress inoculation training. Stress inoculation training, whether done alone or as part of a comprehensive therapy program, provides a helpful toolkit for increasing resilience, improving coping abilities, and fostering psychological well-being.

Stress inoculation training can help people learn coping skills to handle anxiety symptoms, panic attacks, and avoidance behaviors. Therapists can help people address their fears, reduce their anxiety, and recover control of their lives by progressively exposing them to fearful situations while teaching them relaxation techniques and cognitive restructuring skills.

In the treatment of depression, stress inoculation training can help people question negative attitudes and beliefs that contribute to feelings of hopelessness, worthlessness, and despair. Therapists can help people develop more adaptive coping mechanisms and resilience in the face of life's problems by teaching them relaxation techniques, problem-solving abilities, and tactics for increasing social support.

In the context of trauma and PTSD, stress inoculation training can assist individuals in developing coping strategies for hyperarousal, intrusive memories, and avoidance behaviours. Therapists can help clients process traumatic experiences, lessen emotional reactivity, and reestablish a sense of safety and control by teaching them relaxation techniques, stress exposure and desensitization exercises, and cognitive restructuring skills.

## Problem-Solving Skills

Problem-solving skills are a broad range of qualities that allow people to effectively recognize, analyze, and resolve problems. Problem-solving is fundamentally a systematic strategy for handling issues, relying on logic, creativity, and critical thinking to produce and assess viable solutions. Whether dealing with academic tasks, workplace initiatives, or personal difficulties, problem-solving abilities are critical to overcoming barriers and attaining desired results.

Problem-solving often comprises multiple critical processes, including:

**1. Problem Identification:** The first stage in problem-solving is to identify and define the issue or challenge at hand. This may entail defining the nature of the problem, describing the desired outcome, and acquiring relevant data to guide the problem-solving process.

**2. Problem Analysis:** Once the problem has been identified, the following stage is to analyze and comprehend its root causes, contributing variables, and potential implications. This may entail breaking down the problem into smaller components, studying patterns and trends, and identifying any impediments or barriers to resolution.

**3. Generation of Solutions:** After analyzing the problem, individuals discuss and develop viable solutions or strategies for dealing with it. This may entail investigating several choices, weighing the benefits and drawbacks of each technique, and assessing their practicality and effectiveness.

**4. Implementation of Solutions:** Once potential solutions have been found, individuals choose and implement the best course of action to solve the problem. This may include creating an action plan, allocating resources, and tracking progress towards the target objective.

**5. Evaluation and Adjustment:** After implementing a solution, people assess its effectiveness and impact, making changes as needed to better outcomes or address unexpected issues. This could include gathering input, measuring outcomes, and refining techniques for future problem-solving efforts.

## Principles of Problem-Solving Skills

Several fundamental ideas and strategies influence problem-solving skills, to encourage successful problem-solving behavior. These ideas are based on the belief that problem-solving is a skill that can be learned and improved through practice and experience. Some fundamental foundations of problem-solving abilities include:

- **Analytical Thinking:** Problem-solving abilities include the capacity to think analytically and critically about situations, breaking them down into smaller components and discovering underlying patterns or trends. Analytical thinking enables people to obtain a better grasp of the problem and devise more effective solutions.
- **Creativity and Innovation:** Effective problem-solving frequently necessitates thinking outside the box and investigating novel solutions to problems. Individuals can produce unique ideas, perspectives, and problem-solving approaches thanks to creativity and innovation, which promotes adaptability and flexibility in the face of uncertainty.
- **Collaboration and Communication:** Collaborating and communicating with others improves problem-solving skills by harnessing multiple perspectives, knowledge, and resources to tackle complex problems. Collaboration promotes teamwork, mutual support, and group problem-solving, resulting in more solid and long-lasting solutions.
- **Persistence and Resilience:** Problem-solving abilities necessitate tenacity

and resilience in the face of setbacks and challenges. Individuals with a growth mindset and a willingness to learn from failure are better able to overcome obstacles, adjust to changing circumstances, and pursue their goals.

- **Continuous Learning and Improvement:** Individuals enhance their problem-solving skills by reflecting on their experiences, gathering feedback, and applying what they've learned to future problem-solving endeavors. A dedication to lifelong learning and self-improvement promotes growth, innovation, and problem-solving expertise.

## Techniques for Improving Problem-Solving Skills

There are numerous approaches and activities that people can use to improve their problem-solving abilities and become more successful issue solvers. These approaches are applicable in a variety of contexts, including academic, professional, and personal settings. Some common approaches for developing problem-solving abilities include:

- **Brainstorming:** Brainstorming is the process of coming up with a huge number of ideas or solutions to an issue quickly and without judgment or evaluation. This strategy promotes creativity and diverse thinking by allowing individuals to consider a wide range of options before deciding on the most promising solution.
- **Mind Mapping:** Mind Mapping is a visual technique that entails drawing a diagram or map to express thoughts, concepts, and relationships connected to an issue or challenge. Mind maps assist individuals in organizing their thoughts, identifying connections between ideas, and developing new insights and perspectives on an issue.
- **Decision Trees:** Decision trees are a structured way of analyzing potential solutions to a problem by taking into account the many outcomes and repercussions of each option. Decision trees assist individuals in weighing the risks and rewards of various courses of action, allowing them to make informed decisions based on objective standards.

- **SWOT Analysis:** SWOT analysis is a strategic planning tool for identifying the strengths, weaknesses, opportunities, and threats connected with an issue or scenario. SWOT analysis assists individuals in evaluating their internal capabilities and external environment, finding potential advantages and challenges to inform their problem-solving strategy.
- **Root Cause Analysis:** Root Cause Analysis is a problem-solving technique that entails determining the underlying reasons or elements that contribute to a problem. Individuals who delve deeper to find the main causes of a problem might design more effective solutions that target the underlying issues rather than just the symptoms.
- **Simulation and Role-Playing:** Simulation and role-playing exercises entail modeling real-world events or circumstances in which people must solve problems or make choices. These exercises allow people to practice problem-solving skills in a secure and controlled environment, gradually building confidence and proficiency.

## Applications for Problem-Solving Skills

Problem-solving abilities have numerous applications in a variety of fields, including education, business, healthcare, and personal growth. Problem-solving abilities are vital for managing the challenges of everyday life, whether they are solving hard mathematics issues, developing new corporate ideas, or resolving interpersonal disagreements. Some common uses of problem-solving abilities include:

- **Academic Success:** Problem-solving abilities are critical for academic success, allowing students to approach difficult assignments, projects, and tests with confidence and expertise. Problem-solving abilities are essential for learning and academic success, ranging from solving arithmetic problems and conducting scientific experiments to writing essays and conducting research.
- **Career Advancement:** Problem-solving abilities are highly valued in the workplace because they help people negotiate complicated challenges,

make educated decisions, and drive innovation and progress. Employers across industries seek out individuals with good problem-solving skills since they are well-positioned for professional progression and leadership roles.

- **Conflict Resolution:** Problem-solving abilities are required for resolving conflicts and disagreements in interpersonal interactions, whether in the job, home, or community. Individuals who approach problems with a problem-solving perspective can discover root causes, communicate effectively, and collaborate to find mutually beneficial solutions.

- **Innovation and Entrepreneurship:** Problem-solving abilities are essential for creativity and entrepreneurship because they allow people to recognize unmet needs, investigate new opportunities, and develop unique solutions to complex challenges. Entrepreneurs with good problem-solving abilities are better prepared to face the obstacles of beginning and growing a business, including product development, marketing, customer service, and operations.

- **Personal Development:** Problem-solving abilities are essential for personal growth and self-improvement, allowing people to overcome hurdles, achieve goals, and manage life's challenges with perseverance and confidence. Individuals can improve their critical thinking, decision-making, and adaptability by developing their problem-solving abilities, resulting in more success and fulfillment in life.

7

# CHAPTER SIX: LIFESTYLE ADJUSTMENTS

## Time Management

In today's fast-paced world, time is a valuable and finite resource that frequently feels like it's slipping away from us. With professional commitments, personal duties, and social obligations, finding time to complete everything we need and want to do can seem impossible. However, efficient time management is the key to recovering control of our schedules, increasing productivity, and lowering stress. living more rewarding lives.

## Understanding Time Management

Time management is essentially the process of planning, organizing, and prioritizing tasks and activities to make the most use of one's time. It entails establishing objectives, allocating resources, and implementing techniques to increase productivity while minimizing waste. Effective time management is working smarter, not harder, and focusing on activities that are consistent with our beliefs, priorities, and long-term goals.

The concept of time management is based on the awareness that time is a finite and non-renewable resource that must be handled carefully. Just as we carefully budget our funds to ensure that we fulfill our financial objectives and obligations, we must likewise budget our time to ensure that it is allocated by our priorities and values. By taking a proactive and intentional approach to time management, we can boost productivity, reduce stress, and free up more time for the things that are most important in our lives.

## Principles of Time Management

Several important ideas and strategies govern effective time management, to increase productivity and balancing work and personal life. These concepts are based on the understanding that time is a limited resource that must be wisely managed to achieve desired results. Here are some basic time management principles:

- **Goal Setting:** Setting goals is an important time management strategy since it gives our efforts direction and purpose. Setting clear, defined, and attainable goals allows us to prioritize things that contribute to our long-term aims while avoiding distractions from less important activities.
- **Prioritization:** Prioritization is the process of determining the most important tasks and activities and allocating time and resources accordingly. By discriminating between urgent and critical jobs and concentrating on high-value activities, we may increase productivity and get better results in less time.
- **Planning and Scheduling:** Planning and scheduling are critical components of effective time management because they allow us to arrange our time in ways that reflect our goals and responsibilities. Creating a schedule, whether through a daily planner, calendar app, or task management software, allows us to stay organized, focused, and on track to achieve our objectives.
- **Time Blocking:** Time blocking is a time management method that involves allocating defined blocks of time to certain tasks or activities. By grouping related tasks and allocating uninterrupted time to focus on them, we can reduce distractions, improve concentration, and increase output.

- **Batching Tasks:** Batching chores entails grouping comparable tasks and executing them in batches rather than individually throughout the day. This strategy reduces the amount of time and mental energy spent switching between activities, which can improve efficiency and production.
- **Setting Boundaries:** Setting boundaries is critical for good time management because it protects our time and energy from being absorbed by unnecessary or time-consuming tasks. Setting boundaries allows us to prioritize self-care and focus on activities that correspond with our goals and beliefs, whether that means limiting work hours, saying no to unneeded commitments, or establishing digital boundaries to reduce distractions.

## Techniques For Effective Time Management

Individuals can use a variety of approaches and strategies to improve their time management abilities and make better use of their time. These strategies can be adjusted to individual preferences and needs. They may include:

1. **The Eisenhower Matrix:** The Eisenhower Matrix, also known as the Urgent-Important Matrix, is a time management tool that allows people to prioritize tasks according to their urgency and importance. Individuals can direct their time and energy towards activities that correspond with their aims and values by categorizing work into four quadrants: urgent and important, important but not urgent, urgent but not important, and neither urgent nor important.
2. **The Pomodoro Technique:** The Pomodoro Technique is a time management technique that divides work into intervals of 25 minutes each, interspersed by short breaks. Individuals who work in focused spurts and take regular pauses can maintain concentration, minimize burnout, and boost output.
3. **The Two-Minute Rule:** The Two-Minute Rule suggests that if a task can be performed in two minutes or less, it should be done right away rather

than put off until later. This strategy helps to keep tiny jobs from piling up and becoming overwhelming, while also encouraging proactive action and efficiency.

4. **Time Tracking:** Time tracking is the process of monitoring and recording how one spends their time throughout the day. Individuals who keep track of their activities and discover time wasters and inefficiencies can make better decisions about how to manage their time and identify areas for improvement.

5. **Task Prioritisation Techniques:** Techniques such as the ABCDE method or the 1-3-5 rule assist individuals in identifying and prioritizing activities based on their importance and urgency. Individuals can improve their achievements by prioritizing work and focusing on high-value activities.

6. **Technology Tools:** Calendar applications, task management software, and productivity apps are examples of technological tools that can assist individuals in organizing their schedules, tracking their activities, and staying on top of deadlines and obligations. These technologies send reminders, messages, and alerts to keep people on track and ensure that nothing slips between the cracks.

## Applications for Time Management

Effective time management has numerous applications in many areas of life, including job, school, relationships, and personal development. Time management skills are critical for success and well-being, whether it's managing deadlines, juggling various obligations, or making time for self-care and relaxation. Some common applications of time management are:

- **office Productivity:** Time management skills are critical for increasing productivity and efficiency in the office. Employees can obtain greater results by prioritizing activities, controlling deadlines, and minimizing distractions.

- **Academic Success:** Time management skills are essential for academic success because they allow students to manage their homework, study efficiently, and meet deadlines. Students can reduce stress, increase scores, and achieve academic goals by managing their time effectively and remaining organized.

- **Stress Reduction:** Effective time management allows people to plan, stay organized, and prevent last-minute hurries and disasters. Individuals who manage their time successfully can achieve a sense of control and predictability in their lives, lowering feelings of overwhelm and worry.

- **Work-Life Balance:** Time management skills are vital for maintaining a healthy work-life balance, allowing people to prioritize their personal and family demands in addition to their professional duties. Individuals who set boundaries, schedule time for self-care and relaxation, and properly manage their workload can experience greater satisfaction and fulfillment in all aspects of their lives.

- **Goal Achievement:** Time management skills are essential for attaining long-term objectives and aspirations. Individuals can work towards their hopes and aspirations one step at a time by breaking down goals into doable tasks, setting deadlines, and taking constant action.

## Work-Life Balance

Work-life balance is defined as the balance between the demands of work and the needs of personal life, which include family, relationships, health, and leisure activities. It entails finding the correct balance of time, energy, and attention to meet tasks and commitments in all domains while also caring for our physical, mental, and emotional well-being. Achieving work-life balance entails integrating work and personal life in such a way that we can thrive in all aspects of our lives.

The concept of work-life balance recognizes that we are multifaceted individuals with demands and interests that extend beyond our professional identities. It emphasizes the necessity of putting self-care, relationships, and personal fulfillment first, followed by work success and achievement. Work-life balance is not a one-size-fits-all idea, but rather a very personal and subjective experience that differs from person to person depending on personality, values, priorities, and life circumstances.

## The Significance of Work-Life Balance

Work-life balance is critical to our general health, happiness, and quality of life. It offers several advantages for our physical, mental, and emotional health, as well as our relationships and overall happiness in life. Work-life balance is crucial for several reasons, including:

1. **Reduced Stress and Burnout:** Maintaining a healthy work-life balance reduces stress and prevents burnout. Chronic stress from overwork and long hours can hurt our physical and mental health, causing weariness, anxiety, and depression. By setting boundaries and scheduling time for relaxation, hobbies, and social activities, we can recharge our batteries and shield ourselves from the detrimental consequences of stress.

2. **Improved Physical Health:** Work-life balance has been linked to better physical health outcomes, including decreased rates of chronic diseases including heart disease, obesity, and diabetes. Balancing work with regular exercise, the right diet, and adequate sleep strengthens our immune system, increases energy, and lowers the chance of disease and damage. Prioritizing self-care and healthy practices improves our general well-being and longevity.

3. **Improved Mental Well-Being:** Work-life balance is critical for our mental and emotional health, as it allows us to retain a positive attitude, cope with adversities, and create resilience. Taking breaks from work, spending time with loved ones, and participating in things that offer us joy and fulfillment all help us feel happier, more satisfied, and fulfilled. We can improve our quality of life by focusing on our mental health.

4. **Stronger Relationships:** Balancing work and personal life promotes deeper and more meaningful connections with family, friends, and loved ones. Spending quality time together, sharing experiences, and making memories develops and deepens friendships, giving us a greater sense of belonging and support. Prioritizing relationships fosters a

sense of fulfillment and purpose that extends beyond our professional accomplishments, contributing to our general happiness and well-being.

5. **Increased Productivity and Creativity:** Work-life balance promotes increased productivity, creativity, and innovation in the workplace. Taking regular breaks, pursuing hobbies, and participating in leisure activities refills our mental energy, boosts attention and concentration, and sharpens our problem-solving abilities. Allowing our thoughts to relax and recharge helps us become more efficient, effective, and inspired at work.

## Challenges of Achieving Work-Life Balance

Despite its importance, maintaining a work-life balance can be difficult in today's hyperconnected and demanding society. Balancing work and personal life is challenging for a variety of reasons, including:

- **Workaholism:** Workaholism is a culture that emphasizes hard hours and sacrifices to achieve professional success. Many people feel compelled to work excessively and prioritize their employment above their personal lives, resulting in imbalances and burnout.
- **Technology and Connectivity:** The advancement of technology and the emergence of remote work have blurred the lines between work and personal life. Constant connectedness via smartphones, email, and social media makes it harder to unplug from work and truly immerse in leisure and relaxation.
- **High Expectations and Perfectionism:** High expectations and perfectionism can lead to individuals pushing themselves to their limits and ignoring their well-being in the pursuit of excellence. Fear of failing or falling short of expectations can lead to excessive work and self-imposed pressure to succeed in many aspects of life.
- **unexpected Work Demands:** Certain professions, such as healthcare, emergency services, and hospitality, require unexpected work schedules and demands, which might disturb the work-life balance. Shift employ-

ment, irregular hours, and on-call responsibilities can make it difficult to maintain consistency and stability in your personal life.

· **Family and Caregiving Responsibilities:** Balancing employment with family and caregiving responsibilities complicates the work-life balance. Managing childcare, eldercare, housework, and personal obligations takes careful planning, coordination, and assistance from family members and carers.

## Strategies to Achieve Work-Life Balance

While establishing a work-life balance may appear difficult, it is possible with deliberate effort, intention, and commitment. We may make our lives more harmonious and enjoyable by using ideas and practices that promote balance and well-being. Here are some practical ideas for establishing work-life balance.

1. **Set Boundaries:** Define specified work hours, unplug from work emails and notifications after those hours, and communicate your availability to coworkers and superiors. Protect your time by prioritizing self-care, leisure, and relaxation.

2. **P.rioritise Self-Care:** Schedule regular breaks, engage in relaxing and rejuvenating activities, and take care of your physical, mental, and emotional wellbeing. Prioritise sleep, nutrition, exercise, and mindfulness techniques to boost your energy and resilience.

3. **Practice Time Management:** Set goals, prioritize work, and organize your schedule to maximize productivity and save lost time. Calendars, to-do lists, and task management apps can help you keep organized and focused on your top objectives.

4. **Delegate and Outsource:** Delegate chores and responsibilities that others can do to free up time and energy for the things that are most important to you. Whether at work or home, identify chores that can be assigned to coworkers, family members, or service providers to lighten your burden and minimize stress.

5. **Effective Communication:** Tell your boss, coworkers, and family members about your wants, priorities, and boundaries openly and honestly. Convey your availability, expectations, and constraints so that everyone understands and respects your time.

6. **Pursue Work-Life Integration:** Rather than seeking an ideal balance between work and personal life, focus on integrating the two in a way that is consistent with your values, objectives, and ambitions. Look for ways to include aspects of your personal life into your workday, such as taking breaks to spend time with loved ones, pursuing hobbies, or practicing self-care.

7. **Set Realistic Expectations:** Manage your expectations and recognize that achieving work-life balance is a continuous journey, not a destination. Be realistic about what you can do in a given day or week, and be willing to alter your goals and priorities as necessary to keep

## Healthy Sleep Habits

Sleep is essential in almost all aspects of our lives. Sleep is when our bodies repair and revitalize themselves, consolidating memories, regulating emotions, and performing critical activities that keep us healthy and working optimally.

1. **Physical Health:** Getting enough sleep is essential for physical health. During sleep, the body heals tissues, produces hormones, and boosts the immune system. Chronic sleep deprivation has been associated with an increased risk of obesity, diabetes, heart disease, and other chronic health problems.

2. **Cognitive Function:** Sleep is necessary for memory consolidation, learning, and problem-solving. Getting enough quality sleep boosts concentration, productivity, and decision-making skills. In contrast, sleep deprivation can impede cognitive function, making it difficult to think properly, absorb information, and make judgments.

**3. Emotional Well-Being:** Sleep helps to regulate emotions and mood. Adequate sleep promotes emotional balance, resilience, and mental wellness. Chronic sleep deprivation has been linked to an increased risk of mood disorders including sadness and anxiety, as well as irritability, mood swings, and emotional instability.

**4. Overall Quality of Life:** Adopting healthy sleep patterns improves one's overall well-being and quality of life. When we receive adequate restful sleep, we wake up feeling refreshed, energized, and prepared to face the day. Poor sleep, on the other hand, can make us feel exhausted, sluggish, and unmotivated, reducing our enjoyment of daily activities and our capacity to fully participate in life.

## Consequences of poor sleeping habits

Unfortunately, many people suffer from poor sleep patterns, whether owing to lifestyle choices, stress, or underlying sleep disorders. Inadequate or poor-quality sleep can have far-reaching repercussions for all aspects of our lives.

1. **Daytime exhaustion:** One of the most visible side effects of insufficient sleep is daytime exhaustion and drowsiness. When we don't get enough sleep or have interrupted sleep, we're more likely to feel weary, lethargic, and unmotivated during the day, making it difficult to concentrate, focus, and do everyday chores properly.

2. **Impaired Cognitive Function:** Sleep deprivation can affect cognitive performance in a variety of ways. It can impair memory consolidation, making it difficult to store and recall knowledge. It can also affect attention, concentration, and decision-making skills, resulting in lower productivity and performance at work or school.

3. **Mood Changes:** Inadequate sleep can have a substantial impact on mood and emotional well-being. Sleep deprivation is associated with increased irritability, mood swings, and emotional instability. Chronic sleep deprivation has also been related to an increased risk of mood

disorders, including despair and anxiety.

4. **Increased Risk of Health Problems:** Poor sleep patterns have been linked to an increased risk of obesity, diabetes, heart disease, and stroke. Sleep deprivation can interfere with the body's hormonal balance, resulting in abnormalities in appetite-regulating hormones and an increased risk of weight gain and metabolic problems.

5. **Weakened Immune System:** Getting enough sleep is vital for a healthy immune system. During sleep, the body creates cytokines, which assist regulate the immune response and fight infections. Chronic sleep deprivation can impair the immune system, making us more vulnerable to ailments like colds, flu, and infections.

6. **Increased Risk of Accidents:** Sleep deprivation can decrease reaction time, judgment, and coordination, increasing the likelihood of accidents and injuries. Drowsy driving, in particular, is a major worry because it can be as deadly as driving while under the influence of alcohol or drugs.

## Practical Advice for Healthy Sleep Habits

Fortunately, there are numerous actions we can take to enhance our sleeping habits and achieve the restorative sleep our bodies require. Here are some practical ways to promote healthy sleep:

- **Maintain a Sleep Schedule:** Try to go to bed and wake up at the same time every day, including weekends. Consistency helps to regulate your body's internal clock, resulting in higher sleep quality.
- **Create a Relaxing Bedtime Routine:** Set up a calm nighttime ritual to communicate to your body that it's time to unwind and prepare for sleep. This could include reading, taking a warm bath, or practicing relaxation techniques like deep breathing or meditation.
- **Create a Comfortable Sleep Environment:** Keep your bedroom dark, quiet, and cool. Invest in a comfy mattress and pillows, and try utilizing white noise machines or earplugs to drown out any sounds.
- **Limit Screen Time Before Bed:** The blue light emitted by screens might

interfere with the body's generation of melatonin, a hormone that regulates sleep and waking cycles. Limit your exposure to displays like cellphones, tablets, and computers in the hour before bedtime.

- **Watch What You Eat and Drink:** Avoid heavy meals, coffee, and alcohol before bedtime because they can impair sleep. Instead, choose light, nutritious snacks and herbal teas that aid in relaxation and digestion.
- **Get Regular Exercise:** Regular physical activity can help you sleep better and longer. Aim for at least 30 minutes of moderate exercise most days of the week, but avoid vigorous exercise near bedtime because it can be stimulating and make it difficult to fall asleep.
- **Manage Stress and Anxiety:** Stress and anxiety can disrupt sleep, so it's critical to find healthy strategies to manage them. Deep breathing, meditation, and progressive muscle relaxation are among the relaxation techniques that can help you calm your mind and body before bedtime.
- **Seek Professional Help if Necessary:** If you're having persistent sleep problems or suspect you have a sleep disorder like insomnia or sleep apnea, don't hesitate to consult a healthcare professional. They can assess your symptoms, make a diagnosis, and suggest relevant treatments.

8

# CHAPTER SEVEN: SOCIAL SUPPORT AND CONNECTION

## Building a Support Network

In life, we all experience problems, failures, and uncertainties that can make us feel overwhelmed, stressed, and alone. Having a solid support network can be extremely beneficial during these times. A support network is made up of people who offer emotional, practical, and occasionally financial assistance during difficult times. These people may include family members, friends, colleagues, mentors, and even professionals like therapists or counselors.

## Understanding the Importance of Support Networks

1. **Emotional Support:** One of the key purposes of a support network is to provide emotional support during difficult times. Whether you're going through a personal crisis, a major life transition, or simply feeling stressed out, having someone to talk to and lean on can make you feel less lonely, alone, and despondent. Emotional support can take many forms, such as extending a sympathetic ear, words of encouragement, or simply being present

73

for someone in need.

**2. Practical Support:** In addition to emotional support, a support network can help with daily activities and responsibilities. This may involve assistance with childcare, transportation, housework, or running errands. Members of a support network can help one other cope with difficult times by sharing the burden of day-to-day obligations.

**3. Validation and Perspective:** A support network can provide validation and perspective during difficult circumstances. When we're dealing with painful emotions or making difficult decisions, it might be beneficial to hear someone else's feedback and viewpoint to help us see things more clearly. Trusted friends, family members, or mentors can offer helpful insights, feedback, and comfort that we are not alone in our challenges.

**4. Stress Reduction:** Research indicates that social support can assist reduce stress and increase general well-being. Knowing that there are people in our lives who care about us and are eager to help and support us can help us cope with the negative impacts of stress and adversity. In times of crisis or uncertainty, having a support network can provide a sense of comfort and stability, allowing us to cope better with life's obstacles.

**5. Increased Resilience:** Having a strong support network can boost our resilience in the face of hardship. When we have others to lean on for support, we are better able to recover from setbacks, overcome barriers, and adjust to change. Knowing that we have a safety net of caring people can boost our confidence and fortitude to face life's obstacles head-on.

## Building a Support Network: Practical Strategies

Begin by recognizing potential sources of assistance in your life. This could include family members, close friends, coworkers, neighbors, or others from your community. Consider who you can trust and confide in, as well as who has already demonstrated reliability and assistance.

1. **Nurture Existing Relationships:** Developing a support network takes time, effort, and commitment in relationships. Spending quality time together, staying in touch regularly, and expressing gratitude to those in your life are all ways to nourish and improve current connections. Small acts of compassion and support can go a long way towards strengthening relationships with others.

2. **Be Open and Vulnerable:** Establishing a support network necessitates vulnerability and transparency. Don't be reluctant to talk about your challenges, anxieties, and doubts with trusted friends or family members. Opening out to others can establish stronger bonds and provide possibilities for empathy, understanding, and support.

3. **Seek Out Like-Minded Communities:** Consider joining groups, clubs, or organizations that share your interests, values, and aspirations. Surrounding yourself with like-minded people, whether through a hobby group, a support group, or a professional network, can give you a sense of belonging and community.

4. **Offer Help to Others:** Creating a support network is a two-way street. Just as you want help from others, you should be willing to provide it in return. Actively listen, encourage people, and be there for them when they are in need. Being a supportive friend or family member will deepen your ties and develop a network of mutual support.

5. **Utilise Technology:** In today's digital age, technology may be a very useful tool for establishing and sustaining a support network. Stay in touch with friends and family via phone conversations, text messaging, social media, or video chats. Virtual support groups and online forums can also provide a sense of belonging and connection, particularly for people who do not have access to local support networks.

6. **Seek Professional Help if Needed:** If you're dealing with mental health concerns, chronic stress, or other severe obstacles, don't be afraid to seek professional assistance. Therapists, counselors, and support groups can provide specialized assistance and direction to help you get through

difficult times and build resilience.

## Maintaining a Support Network: Tips for Long-Term Success

- **Communicate Openly and Honestly:** Effective communication is critical for maintaining healthy relationships in a support network. Be upfront and honest with your friends and family about your needs, limitations, and expectations. If anything bothers you or causes friction in a relationship, discuss it freely and gently.
- **Set boundaries:** Boundaries are essential for maintaining healthy relationships and avoiding burnout. Be clear about your boundaries and priorities, and don't be hesitant to decline requests or demands that are beyond your capabilities. Setting limits demonstrates self-respect and signals to others how to effectively help you.
- **Practice Active Listening:** Active listening is an essential ability in every healthy relationship. Active listening is paying full attention to the person speaking, asking clarifying questions, and validating their thoughts and experiences. Demonstrate understanding and compassion, and avoid offering advice or answers unless specifically requested.
- **Express Gratitude and Appreciation:** Thank others for their help. A simple thank you or a heartfelt expression of appreciation can enhance relationships and reinforce positive behavior. Let others know how much their help means to you, and they will be more likely to help you again.
- **Stay Connected:** To preserve solid relationships, check in with members of your support network regularly. Whether it's a quick phone call, a text message, or a face-to-face visit, being connected fosters relationships and ensures that your support network is robust and reliable.

## Effective Communication Skills

Effective communication is more than just transmitting information; it is about making genuine relationships and establishing mutual understanding among individuals. It requires verbal and nonverbal communication, as well as active listening and empathy. Effective communicators can express themselves clearly and confidently, change their communication style to suit diverse audiences, and actively engage with people to establish rapport and trust.

## The Value of Effective Communication

1. **Building Stronger Relationships:** Effective communication is critical to developing stronger, more meaningful relationships with people. When we speak openly, honestly, and respectfully, we foster a culture of trust and reciprocal respect, which enriches our relationships with family, friends, coworkers, and peers.

2. **Resolving Conflicts:** Conflicts and disagreements are unavoidable in any relationship or job context. However, excellent communication skills can assist in navigating issues constructively and reaching mutually beneficial outcomes. People can overcome problems and preserve strong relationships by attentively listening, expressing their emotions quietly, and seeking compromise.

3. **Improving Collaboration and Teamwork:** Effective communication is essential for encouraging collaboration and teamwork in professional contexts. When team members can communicate clearly and honestly, they may exchange ideas, coordinate efforts, and collaborate more successfully to achieve common objectives.

4. **Improving Leadership Skills:** Effective communication is a key characteristic of effective leadership. Leaders who communicate clearly, inspire trust, and listen empathetically are more effective at motivating and engaging their teams, fostering innovation, and driving organizational success.

5. **Advancing Career Success:** Effective communication skills are highly recognized in the workplace and can have a substantial impact on an individual's professional success. Effective communicators excel in delivering presentations, participating in meetings, and negotiating with clients.

## Key Features of Effective Communication Skills

- **Clarity and Conciseness:** Effective communicators communicate themselves clearly and concisely, using basic language and avoiding jargon or technical phrases that others may misunderstand. They organize their thoughts logically and frame their message in an easy-to-follow and understandable format.

- **Active Listening:** Active listening is an important part of good communication. It is thoroughly engaging with the speaker, paying attention to both verbal and nonverbal signs, and attempting to comprehend their viewpoint and emotions. Effective listeners avoid interrupting, provide feedback, and ask clarifying questions to ensure they receive the speaker's message correctly.

- **Empathy and Understanding:** Empathy is the ability to comprehend and share other people's emotions. Effective communicators show empathy by identifying others' emotions, validating their experiences, and reacting with compassion and understanding. Communicators who demonstrate empathy generate trust and rapport with others, resulting in a helpful and inclusive environment.

- **Nonverbal Communication:** Body language, facial expressions, and tone of voice all play an important role in efficient communication. Effective communicators pay attention to nonverbal indicators and ensure that their body language and tone match their vocal message. They also evaluate nonverbal signs from others to obtain insight into their thoughts and emotions.

- **Assertiveness:** Assertiveness is the ability to convey one's opinions, feelings, and desires openly and confidently, without being aggressive or passive. Effective communicators are confident in expressing their thoughts and arguing for their rights while respecting the rights and opinions of others. They assert themselves respectfully and assertively which fosters mutual understanding and respect.

- **Adaptability:** Effective communicators can tailor their communication style to different audiences and situations. They understand that communication preferences differ depending on cultural background, personality, and environment, therefore they tailor their approach accordingly. Communicators that are flexible and adaptable may ensure that their message reaches their intended audience and achieves the desired result.

## Practical strategies for improving communication skills

- **Practice Active Listening:** Make an effort to actively listen to others during conversations. Concentrate on the speaker, keep eye contact, and refrain from interrupting. Summarise what you've heard and ask clarifying questions to ensure comprehension.
- **Be Clear and Concise:** When sharing your views and ideas, aim for clarity and concision. Avoid using needless jargon or convoluted terminology, and keep your thoughts clear and coherent. Be attentive to your audience and customize your message to their level of comprehension.
- **Empathy and Understanding:** Use empathy and understanding in your interactions with others. Recognize their emotions and experiences, and respond with empathy and kindness. Offer support and encouragement rather than judgment or criticism.
- **Monitor Your Nonverbal Cues:** When speaking with people, be aware of your body language, facial expressions, and tone of voice. Ensure that your nonverbal clues reflect your vocal statement and express openness, confidence, and respect.
- **Practice Assertiveness:** Practice assertiveness by honestly and confidently expressing your opinions, feelings, and desires. Use "I" sentences to express yourself properly and assertively, and avoid confrontational or passive communication methods. To boost confidence and assertiveness, practice assertive communication in a variety of settings.
- **Seek comments:** Ask for comments from others on your communication skills and areas for growth. Ask trusted friends, coworkers, or mentors for candid input on your communication approach, and be willing to accept constructive criticism. Use feedback to learn and improve as a communicator.

- **Take Communication Skills Training:** Consider taking a communication skills training course or workshop to help you improve your communication abilities even more. These programs frequently include practical suggestions, tactics, and exercises to improve communication effectiveness in a variety of circumstances.

## Seeking Professional Help

**1. Access to Expertise:** Mental health specialists such as therapists, counselors, psychiatrists, and psychologists have specialized training and experience in diagnosing and treating mental health issues. They can offer evidence-based therapies, therapy, and medication management that are tailored to each individual's specific requirements and circumstances.

**2. validity and Support:** Seeking professional care for mental health issues can provide validity and support to people who are experiencing loneliness, isolation, or humiliation. Mental health practitioners provide a safe, nonjudgmental environment in which individuals can communicate their thoughts, feelings, and experiences without fear of stigma or prejudice.

**3. Personalized Treatment Plans:** Mental health experts collaborate with their clients to create personalized treatment plans that address their unique requirements, goals, and preferences. Professionals personalize their approach to assist people reach their best mental health and well-being, whether through talk therapy, cognitive-behavioral approaches, medication management, or other interventions.

**4. Crisis Intervention:** In times of crisis or extreme distress, mental health experts can offer rapid assistance and intervention to help people cope with overwhelming emotions and thoughts. Crisis hotlines, emergency psychiatric services, and crisis intervention teams are accessible 24 hours a day, seven days a week to help and connect people with the resources and care they need.

**5. Building Coping Skills:** Mental health specialists educate people on how to manage stress, regulate emotions, and deal with difficult situations effectively. Individuals discover healthy strategies to cope with life's ups and downs through therapy and counseling, developing resilience and laying a solid basis for long-term mental well-being.

**6. Prevention and Early Intervention:** Seeking professional care for mental health concerns can help prevent the emergence of more serious mental health issues and promote early intervention when problems arise. Individuals can improve their overall quality of life by addressing mental health difficulties as soon as they arise.

## Barriers to Seeking Professional Help

Despite the numerous benefits of receiving professional care for mental health issues, people may face several obstacles that keep them from seeking help. Some such barriers are:

- **Stigma and Shame:** The stigma associated with mental illness can discourage people from getting care for fear of being judged, misunderstood, or labeled as "weak" or "crazy." Stigma can stem from societal attitudes, cultural beliefs, or even internalized self-judgment, making it difficult for people to admit their problems and seek help.
- **Financial Barriers:** For many people, the cost of mental health services is a substantial barrier to receiving them. Therapy and counseling sessions can be costly, and not everyone has access to reasonably priced mental health care or enough insurance coverage. Financial considerations may stop people from requesting assistance, even if they recognize the need for it.
- **Little access to care:** Some communities, particularly rural or underserved ones, may have little or no access to mental health care. There could be a dearth of mental health specialists, excessive wait times for appointments, or limited transportation alternatives, making it difficult for people to get

the care they require.

- **Fear of Judgement or Rejection:** People who are afraid of being judged or rejected by friends, family members, or employers may avoid seeking help for mental health issues. They may be concerned about how others may see them, as well as potential negative outcomes such as social stigma, discrimination, or job loss.
- **Cultural and Language Barriers:** Cultural and cultural limitations might make it difficult to obtain professional care for mental health issues. Some people may originate from cultures where mental illness is stigmatized or considered taboo, making it difficult for them to open up about their issues or seek help. Language problems can also impede communication and reduce access to culturally appropriate care.

## Strategies for Overcoming Barriers to Getting Professional Help

1. **Normalise Mental Health Conversations:** Encourage open, honest discussions about mental health and well-being to remove stigma and raise awareness. Normalise seeking assistance for mental health issues by sharing personal experiences, teaching others about mental illness, and fostering a supportive and non-judgmental environment.

2. **Provide Education and Resources:** Inform people about the benefits of obtaining professional help for mental health issues, as well as information on accessible resources and services. Provide workshops, seminars, or instructional sessions on stress management, coping strategies, and seeking mental health care.

3. **Promote Accessibility and Affordability:** Advocate for increased access to inexpensive mental health services, as well as mental health insurance coverage. Look into low-cost or sliding-scale treatment programs, community mental health centers, or internet counseling platforms that provide affordable alternatives to traditional therapy.

4. **Offer Support and Encouragement:** Provide support and encouragement to people who are hesitant to seek professional care for mental health issues. Listen empathetically, affirm their feelings, and reassure them

that it is acceptable to seek assistance. Encourage them to make baby efforts towards finding help, and volunteer to accompany them to appointments if necessary.

5. **Address Cultural and Linguistic Barriers:** Identify and address cultural and linguistic barriers to receiving professional mental health care. Provide culturally competent care by providing services in different languages, connecting with varied populations, and respecting cultural beliefs and practices about mental health.

6. **Normalise Help-Seeking Behaviours:** Model good coping methods, seek help when necessary, and emphasize the value of self-care and well-being. Create a caring and inclusive environment in which people may share their opinions and feelings without fear of being judged or stigmatized.

9

# CHAPTER EIGHT: SELF-CARE PRACTICES

## Self-Compassion and Acceptance

Throughout our lives, we frequently face difficulties, disappointments, and self-doubts. During these trying circumstances, it's tempting to be critical of ourselves, pass harsh judgment on ourselves, and hold ourselves to impossible perfection standards. However, practicing self-compassion and acceptance can be a powerful antidote to this inner conflict, allowing us to embrace kindness, understanding, and forgiveness for ourselves.

## Understanding Self-compassion and Acceptance

Self-compassion is defined as the discipline of treating oneself with love, care, and understanding, particularly during times of adversity or pain. It entails realizing our humanity, accepting our flaws, and showing ourselves the same compassion as we would a friend in need. Self-acceptance, on the other hand, is recognizing and accepting all aspects of oneself, including strengths, shortcomings, and flaws, without judgment or self-criticism.

## The significance of self-compassion and acceptance.

1. **Improved Mental Health:** Studies have found that self-compassion is closely linked to increased emotional well-being, decreased levels of anxiety and sadness, and improved overall life satisfaction. Self-compassion and acceptance can help us achieve better inner peace, resilience, and self-esteem.

2. **Reduced Stress and Burnout:** Self-compassion protects against stress and burnout by encouraging a kinder, more loving attitude towards oneself. When we treat ourselves with love and understanding, we are better able to deal with life's obstacles and failures without feeling overwhelmed or depleted.

3. **Improved Relationships:** Practicing self-compassion and acceptance can help us improve our relationships with others. When we are nicer and more tolerant of ourselves, we are better equipped to express genuine empathy, compassion, and understanding to others. This leads to stronger connections, increased intimacy, and more meaningful relationships.

4. **Greater Resilience:** Self-compassion and acceptance are essential components of resilience, which is the ability to recover from adversity and grow stronger in the face of hardships. By accepting our flaws and treating ourselves with care, we increase our emotional flexibility and adaptability, allowing us to manage life's ups and downs with greater ease and grace.

5. **Enhanced Self-Regulation:** Self-compassion and acceptance are linked to better self-regulation and emotional intelligence. When we are compassionate towards ourselves, we are better able to control our emotions, handle stress, and make healthier decisions in our lives.

# Practical Strategies for Developing Self-Compassion and Acceptance.

Mindfulness entails being present at the moment, free of judgment or attachment to our thoughts and feelings. Mindfulness meditation can help us develop self-compassion and acceptance by helping us to notice our thoughts and feelings with inquiry and kindness, rather than reacting with criticism or resistance.

- **Challenge Negative Self-Talk:** Listen to your inner conversation and respond with self-compassion. Instead of berating yourself for perceived flaws or failures, show yourself kindness, encouragement, and understanding. Treat yourself like a cherished friend in need.
- **Cultivate Self-Kindness:** Actively look for opportunities to be kind to yourself in little, everyday ways. This could include making time for self-care activities that nourish your body, mind, and soul, such as taking a bath, going for a stroll in nature, or engaging in a pastime you enjoy. Treat yourself with the same care and concern that you would give to a loved one.
- **Practice Forgiveness:** Forgive yourself for your past mistakes, regrets, and resentments. Recognize that you are human, and like everyone else, you will make mistakes and face setbacks from time to time. Instead of obsessing over previous mistakes, concentrate on learning and development, and forgive yourself for being imperfect.
- **Develop Self-Compassionate Affirmations:** Create a list of self-compassionate affirmations or mantras that speak to you, and repeat them frequently to establish a compassionate mindset. Some examples of affirmations are "I am worthy of love and acceptance just as I am," "I forgive myself for past mistakes and embrace my imperfections," as well as "I am deserving of kindness and compassion."
- **Seek Support and Connection:** For encouragement and validation, contact friends, family, or support groups. Sharing your challenges with others might help normalize your feelings and remind you that you are not alone

in your quest for self-compassion and acceptance. Surround yourself with individuals who will encourage and support you on your journey to healing and progress.

- **Practice Gratitude:** Develop a grateful attitude by focusing on the good things in your life and acknowledging your blessings, no matter how small. Gratitude can help you transform your viewpoint from self-criticism and scarcity to self-compassion and abundance, helping you to better appreciate yourself and your life.

## Hobbies and Leisure Activities

Hobbies and leisure activities refer to a wide range of interests, occupations, and pastimes that people engage in for enjoyment, relaxation, and personal fulfillment. They can take many different forms, including creative endeavors like painting, writing, or performing music, outdoor activities like hiking, gardening, or birdwatching, and social hobbies like cooking, crafting, or playing sports. Hobbies and leisure activities are distinguished by their voluntary nature, meaning they are done for pleasure rather than obligation or need.

## The Value of Hobbies and Leisure Activities

1. **Stress Reduction:** Hobbies and recreational activities provide much-needed relief from the tensions and pressures of everyday life. It lets people take a break from work, housework, and other duties and engage in activities that provide them joy, relaxation, and a sense of accomplishment. Hobbies provide stress reduction by lowering cortisol levels, reducing anxiety, and promoting a sense of serenity and well-being.

2. **Enhanced Creativity:** Hobbies and leisure activities boost creativity and imagination by giving people a place to express themselves and explore new ideas. Whether it's painting, writing, gardening, or making, creative endeavors allow people to unleash their creativity, experiment with

new ideas, and express themselves in important ways. Creative hobbies promote a state of flow, or "being in the zone," in which people lose track of time and get completely immersed in the action at hand.

3. **Improved Mental Health:** Studies have found that hobbies and leisure activities are related to better mental health outcomes, such as fewer symptoms of sadness, anxiety, and stress. Engaging in fun and meaningful activities improves mood, enhances emotions of happiness and fulfillment, and gives people a sense of purpose and meaning in life. Hobbies are a kind of self-care that promotes relaxation, enjoyment, and personal growth.

4. **Physical Health Benefits:** Many hobbies and recreational pursuits provide physical health benefits as well. Physical activity, whether it's going for a walk, doing yoga, or playing sports, improves cardiovascular health, strengthens muscles and bones, and boosts general fitness and well-being. Physical hobbies also encourage people to stay active, maintain a healthy weight, and adopt health-promoting habits.

5. **Social Connection:** Hobbies and leisure activities allow people to interact with one another and engage with their communities. Hobbies, such as joining a reading club, playing sports, or taking a painting class, allow people to interact with others who share their interests, make friendships, and build supportive social networks. Social activities promote a sense of belonging and camaraderie, which reduces feelings of loneliness and isolation while also enhancing mental and emotional health.

6. **Personal Growth and Development:** Hobbies and leisure activities encourage people to venture outside of their comfort zones, learn new skills, and pursue their passions. Hobbies promote self-discovery, self-expression, and self-improvement by allowing people to pursue their interests, develop talents, and establish a feeling of identity and purpose. Hobbies also promote lifelong learning and curiosity, which aids intellectual development and cognitive function.

# Practical Strategies to Incorporate Hobbies and Leisure Activities

- **Identify Your Interests:** Begin by examining your interests, passions, and curiosities to discover prospective hobbies and leisure activities that appeal to you. Consider what activities make you happy, energized, and alive. Consider previous activities you enjoyed or interests you've always wanted to try but never had the opportunity to explore.

- **Make Time for Hobbies:** Schedule time for hobbies and leisure activities in your calendar, just like you would for work, chores, or other obligations. Set aside time each day or week to do activities that bring you joy and relaxation. Treat hobbies as non-negotiable meetings with yourself, and keep your commitment to self-care and personal fulfillment.

- **Start Small:** If you're new to hobbies or feel intimidated by the prospect of trying anything new, start small and gradually incorporate hobbies into your life. Begin by experimenting with several hobbies on a trial basis, gradually increasing your level of commitment as you discover what works for you.

- **Create a Supportive Environment:** Set up an environment that fosters and supports the pursuit of hobbies and leisure activities. Create a separate room in your home for creative or physical hobbies. Surround yourself with tools, materials, and resources that inspire and motivate you to pursue your hobbies passionately and enthusiastically.

- **Diverse Activities:** Be willing to try a variety of hobbies and leisure activities, particularly those beyond your comfort zone or area of competence. Do not be hesitant to try new things, take risks, and accept failure as part of the learning process. Allow yourself to explore, play, and discover new passions and interests along the road.

- **Connect with Others:** Look for ways to connect with people who share your interests and passions. Join clubs, groups, or online communities dedicated to your hobbies, and take part in social events, workshops, or classes connected to your interests. Making relationships with like-minded people increases the fun and fulfillment you get from your interests while also instilling a sense of belonging and community.

- **Practice Self-Compassion:** Be nice and sympathetic to yourself as you discover and participate in hobbies and leisure activities. Accept imperfections, failures, and obstacles as normal components of the learning process, and treat yourself with tolerance, understanding, and forgiveness along the way. Remember that hobbies should be pleasurable and fulfilling, not a cause of stress or pressure.

# Nutrition and Hydration

Nutrition is the process of extracting and using nutrients from food to promote the growth, repair, and maintenance of the body's tissues and organs. These nutrients include macronutrients such as carbs, proteins, and fats, as well as micronutrients like vitamins and minerals. Hydration, on the other hand, is the consumption of fluids, primarily water, to maintain adequate fluid balance and sustain cellular activity.

## The importance of nutrition and hydration

1. **Optimal Physical Health:** Proper nutrition and hydration are critical for maintaining good physical health and energy. Nutrient-dense diets supply the energy and structural components required for cellular metabolism, tissue repair, and immunological function. Adequate hydration supports optimal fluid balance, electrolyte levels, and tissue hydration, all of which are necessary for cardiovascular health, body temperature regulation, and organ function.

2. **Enhanced Cognitive Function:** Proper nutrition and water are essential for brain health and cognitive function. The brain needs a consistent supply of nutrients and oxygen to function properly, and dehydration or dietary deficits can affect cognitive ability, focus, and memory. A balanced diet high in brain-boosting nutrients including omega-3 fatty acids, antioxidants, and B vitamins promotes cognitive function and mental clarity.

3. **Improved Mood and Emotional Well-Being:** Nutrition and hydration

play a significant role in mood and emotional well-being. Certain nutrients, including omega-3 fatty acids, magnesium, and vitamin D, help to produce neurotransmitters and hormones that regulate mood, stress response, and emotional stability. Staying hydrated and nourished promotes healthy neurotransmitter activity, lowering the risk of mood disorders including depression and anxiety.

4. **Enhanced Athletic Performance:** Proper nutrition and hydration are critical for athletes and active people looking to improve their performance, endurance, and recovery. Carbohydrates are the primary fuel source for exercise, while proteins aid in muscle repair and growth. Hydration is essential for maintaining fluid balance, avoiding dehydration, and controlling body temperature while exercising. Consuming electrolyte-rich beverages, such as sports drinks, can help replenish electrolytes lost through sweat and keep you hydrated during strenuous exercise.

5. **Disease Prevention and Management:** A well-balanced diet and enough hydration are key factors in avoiding chronic diseases like obesity, diabetes, cardiovascular disease, and some types of cancer. A diet high in fruits, vegetables, whole grains, lean meats, and healthy fats contains critical nutrients and antioxidants that boost immune function, lower inflammation, and protect against oxidative stress. Staying hydrated improves kidney function, assists digestion, and helps remove toxins from the body, lowering the risk of urinary tract infections and kidney stones.

## Practical Strategies to Maintain Nutrition and Hydration

- **Consume a Balanced Diet:** Include a range of nutrient-dense foods from all dietary groups, such as fruits, vegetables, whole grains, lean proteins, and healthy fats. Fill your plate with a variety of fruits and vegetables to guarantee a balanced intake of vitamins, minerals, and antioxidants. To encourage muscle repair and growth, eat lean proteins such as poultry, fish, beans, and tofu. Choose whole grains like brown rice, quinoa, and oats over processed grains to get more fiber and minerals.

- **Stay Hydrated:** Drink enough fluids throughout the day to keep your body hydrated and functioning properly. Aim to drink 8-10 glasses of water every day, or more if you're physically active or live in a hot environment. Keep a reusable water bottle with you wherever you go to make it easier to remain hydrated all day. Monitor your urine color to determine your hydration level; pale yellow pee suggests adequate hydration, whereas dark yellow urine may indicate dehydration.

- **Balance Macronutrients:** Include a variety of carbohydrates, proteins, and fats in your meals to give long-lasting energy and satiety. Carbohydrates are the body's principal fuel source, accounting for 45-65% of total daily calories. Choose complex carbs like whole grains, fruits, and vegetables to give fiber and nutrients while also stabilizing blood sugar levels. Poultry, fish, eggs, and lentils are good sources of lean protein that can help with muscle recovery. Consume healthy fats from avocados, nuts, seeds, and olive oil to promote heart health and cognitive function.

- **Portion Control:** Pay attention to portion proportions and eat mindfully to avoid overeating and increase satiety. Use smaller dishes and bowls to help regulate portion sizes and prevent mindless nibbling. Listen to your body's hunger and fullness cues and stop eating when you're content, not when you're too full. Concentrate on savoring each bite and enjoying the flavors and textures of your meals.

- **Plan and Prepare Meals:** Take the time to plan and prepare nutritious meals and snacks ahead of time to help you maintain healthy eating habits throughout the week. Set aside time each week to plan meals, make a grocery list, and prepare components such as fruits, vegetables, and lean proteins. Cook meals in bulk and separate them into containers for convenient grab-and-go options on busy days. Having nutritious meals and snacks readily available lessens the temptation to eat convenience foods or fast food.

- **Read food labels.** When grocery shopping, pay attention to food labels and ingredient lists to make informed decisions about what you eat. Look for items that are low in added sugars, salt, and harmful fats but high in fiber, vitamins, and minerals. When feasible, choose whole, minimally processed foods over highly processed foods that have a high concentration of artificial additives, preservatives, and harmful components.

- **Listen to Your Body:** Pay attention to your body's hunger and fullness signals, and eat intuitively to meet your unique needs and preferences. Respect your cravings and preferences while attempting to make balanced, nutritious choices that promote your health and well-being. Use self-compassion and flexibility while making food choices, and avoid rigorous dietary guidelines or restrictive eating patterns that can lead to feelings of guilt or deprivation.

# 10

# CHAPTER NINE: STRESS MANAGEMENT AT WORK

## Setting Boundaries

Setting boundaries is vital for maintaining successful relationships and protecting our well-being. Boundaries define the limitations and expectations we set in our interactions with others, contributing to a sense of safety, respect, and autonomy. Setting and maintaining boundaries with family members, friends, coworkers, or love partners is essential for building mutual understanding, communication, and trust.

## Understanding Boundaries

Boundaries are the invisible borders we build around ourselves to define what constitutes acceptable and unacceptable behavior in our relationships. They serve as standards for how we expect to be treated by others and how we will react to various situations. Boundaries can be physical, emotional, or relational, and they may include constraints on time, space, communication, and behavior. Healthy boundaries are flexible, clear, and considerate of both our own and others' needs.

## Importance of Setting Boundaries

1. **Self-Respect and Autonomy:** Setting boundaries allows us to assert our needs, preferences, and values in our dealings with others. When we set boundaries, we tell others that we have the right to our thoughts, feelings, and boundaries and that we expect to be treated with dignity and respect.

2. **Healthy Relationships:** Setting boundaries is vital for developing healthy relationships based on mutual respect, trust, and understanding. Clear boundaries help to define a relationship's parameters, establish behavioral expectations, and avoid misunderstandings or confrontations. Healthy limits provide a sense of safety and consistency, making both parties feel secure and valued in the relationship.

3. **Emotional Well-Being:** Setting boundaries is essential for safeguarding our emotional health and avoiding burnout, resentment, and emotional tiredness. When we set boundaries, we create room for self-care, relaxation, and recharging, allowing us to prioritize our own needs rather than overextending ourselves to fulfill the demands of others.

4. **Personal Development and Empowerment:** Setting boundaries is an empowering act that helps us to take charge of our lives and make decisions that reflect our values and priorities. By declaring our limits, we demonstrate our agency and self-determination, which fosters a higher sense of self-confidence, assertiveness, and resilience in the face of adversity.

5. **Conflict Resolution:** Clear boundaries make it easier to resolve issues courteously and constructively. When boundaries are infringed or crossed, it allows for open communication, negotiation, and compromise, resulting in a better understanding and resolution of conflict.

## Challenges in Boundary Setting

- **Fear of Rejection or Abandonment:** Setting boundaries is often difficult due to the fear of rejection or abandonment by others. We may be concerned that asserting our boundaries would result in confrontation, condemnation, or loss of love or affection from others. Overcoming this anxiety means acknowledging our underlying worth and value, regardless of how others react or respond.

- **Guilt or responsibility:** Feelings of guilt or responsibility might impair our capacity to successfully create boundaries. We may feel guilty about prioritizing our own needs over those of others or limiting our time and energy. Setting boundaries is not selfish; rather, it is an act of self-care and self-preservation that benefits both parties in a relationship in the long run.

- **Lack of Assertiveness:** Some people struggle to be aggressive when it comes to setting boundaries because they are afraid of coming across as harsh, selfish, or confrontational. Developing assertiveness skills entails learning to communicate, respectfully, and confidently, as well as arguing for our own needs and boundaries without using aggressiveness or animosity.

- **Boundary Violations:** Another issue in boundary setting is coping with boundary violations from others. Whether deliberate or inadvertent, boundary infractions can be harmful to relationships. To avoid repeated breaches, we must confront boundary violations assertively and openly, clearly articulating our discomfort and enforcing our limits.

## Practical Strategies for Setting Boundaries

- **Identify Your Requirements:** Begin by determining your requirements, values, and priorities in various aspects of your life, such as your job, relationships, and personal time. Consider what is essential to you and which behaviors or situations make you feel uncomfortable or disrespected.

- **Communicate Clearly:** State your boundaries clearly, directly, and assertively, utilizing "I" phrases to express your requirements and preferences. Be precise about what behaviors you consider acceptable and inappropriate, and explain your reasons for setting limits if necessary.

- **Be Consistent:** Consistency is essential for preserving boundaries over time. Once you've established your boundaries, stick to them consistently and strongly whenever they're violated. Avoid making exceptions or allowing boundary infractions to go unchecked, since this can weaken your credibility and confidence in your relationships.

- **Practice Self-Compassion:** Be patient and compassionate with yourself as you work through the process of setting and maintaining boundaries. Recognize that boundary-setting is a skill that requires time and effort to master, and be patient with yourself as you learn to assert your demands and prioritize your well-being.

- **Seek Help:** Seek assistance from trusted friends, family members, or a therapist who can provide encouragement, direction, and affirmation as you struggle to develop and maintain appropriate boundaries. Surround yourself with individuals who respect and support your limits while also providing a safe area for you to communicate your needs and concerns.

- **Set repercussions:** Convey the repercussions for boundary violations and follow through on them if necessary. Consequences should be appropriate to the seriousness of the boundary breach and can range from a mild reminder or explanation of boundaries to more significant acts such as limiting contact or terminating a relationship.

- **Practice Self-Care:** Prioritise self-care and self-compassion when you negotiate boundaries in your relationships. Make time for activities that nourish and renew you, such as exercise, meditation, hobbies, or spending time with loved ones who understand and support your boundaries.

## Benefits of Establishing Healthy Boundaries

- **Improved Self-Esteem and Confidence:** Setting and keeping limits boost self-esteem and confidence by confirming our worth and value as people. When we prioritize our needs and set boundaries, we communicate to ourselves and others that we deserve to be treated with decency and respect.

- **Increased Emotional Resilience:** Healthy boundaries promote emotional resilience by shielding us from harmful or depleting relationships and circumstances. When we set clear boundaries, we create a barrier against negativity, manipulation, and emotional injury, helping us to retain our emotional health and inner serenity.

- **Enhanced Relationships:** Healthy boundaries help to create healthier, more rewarding relationships based on mutual respect, trust, and understanding. When both sides in a relationship respect each other's limits, it fosters a sense of safety, openness, and authenticity, allowing the relationship to flourish and expand.

- **Increased Productivity and Effectiveness:** Setting boundaries allows us to focus our time and energy on things that are meaningful and important to us, enhancing productivity and effectiveness in both personal and professional settings. By defining boundaries for our time, space, and resources, we may direct our efforts toward projects that are consistent with our goals and values, resulting in more success and fulfillment.

- **Reduced Stress and Anxiety:** Healthy boundaries help us feel more in control and predictable in our lives, which reduces stress and anxiety. When we have clear boundaries, we feel empowered to assert our needs and make decisions that benefit our well-being, lessening the sense of overload and ambiguity that can lead to stress and anxiety.

- **Enhanced Personal Growth:** Setting and keeping limits is a strong stimulant for personal development and discovery. As we learn to articulate our wants, values, and priorities in relationships, we get a better awareness of ourselves and what is important to us. Boundary-setting requires us to move outside of our comfort zones, address our anxieties and vulnerabilities, and develop a stronger sense of self-awareness and honesty.

## Seeking Organizational Support

Organizational support refers to a wide range of tools, programs, and interventions that aim to empower individuals and improve their performance, well-being, and satisfaction inside an organization. This support can come in a variety of forms, including:

1. **Mentorship and Coaching:** Connecting individuals with experienced mentors or coaches who can offer direction, counsel, and support as they embark on personal or professional journeys.

2. **Training and Development Programmes:** We provide training sessions, workshops, and educational programs to help people learn new skills, expand their knowledge, and advance their careers.

3. **Employee Assistance Programmes (EAPs):** Offers counselling, mental health services, and wellness tools to help employees' emotional and psychological well-being.

4. **Flexible Work Arrangements:** Provide employees with flexible work hours, telecommuting choices, and other concessions to assist them manage their professional and personal responsibilities.

5. **Financial Assistance and Advantages:** Offering financial assistance, scholarships, tuition reimbursement, and other advantages to help employees achieve their educational or personal development goals.

6. **Networking and Community Building:** Creating networking opportunities, community activities, and affinity groups to assist individuals in connecting with peers, developing relationships, and accessing support networks.

## Importance of Seeking Organisational Support

1. **Access to Resources and Expertise:** Organisational support gives individuals access to valuable resources, expertise, and opportunities that they would not be able to obtain on their own. Organizational support, whether in the form of mentorship, training from a seasoned expert, or financial assistance for additional education, can open doors and extend opportunities for personal and professional development.

2. **Enhanced Performance and Productivity:** Organizations may improve

their performance and productivity by giving employees the tools, training, and support they need to succeed. Employees who feel encouraged and empowered are more driven, engaged, and committed to meeting their objectives and contributing to the organization's success.

3. **Improved Well-being and Satisfaction:** Organizational support improves employees' overall well-being and job satisfaction by addressing their needs, decreasing stress, and encouraging work-life balance. Employees who feel supported and valued by their employer are more likely to report work satisfaction, loyalty, and retention.

4. **Professional Development and Growth:** Seeking organisational support can help people learn new skills, broaden their knowledge, and advance in their jobs. Whether through mentorship, training programs, or networking opportunities, organizational assistance offers individuals the resources and encouragement they require to advance in their professions.

5. **Resilience and adaptability:** Organisational support assists individuals in developing resilience and adaptability in the face of obstacles and failures. Organizations empower individuals by offering a supportive environment and access to resources, allowing them to overcome hurdles, learn from setbacks, and come back stronger.

## Challenges in Seeking Organisational Support

- **Lack of Awareness:** One typical barrier to obtaining organizational support is a lack of knowledge or comprehension of the resources and programs available. Individuals may be unaware of their organization's support services or how to obtain them.

- **Fear of Stigma or Judgement:** Some people may be hesitant to seek organizational support for fear of being stigmatized or judged by coworkers or bosses. They may be concerned about being viewed as incompetent, weak, or unable to handle their obligations.

- **Perceived Barriers to Access:** Complex application processes, confidentiality concerns, or bureaucratic red tape can dissuade people from seeking organisational assistance. They may feel overwhelmed or dismayed by the possibility of overcoming these obstacles.

- **Limited Resource Availability:** In some situations, organizations may have insufficient resources or support programs, making it difficult for individuals to obtain the aid they require. This might be especially difficult in smaller organizations or during times of financial constraints.
- **Cultural or Organizational Norms:** Cultural or organizational standards may hinder people from seeking help or expressing their problems. In some cultures or workplaces, requesting help or acknowledging vulnerability may carry a stigma.

## Practical Strategies to Seek Organisational Support

- **Educate Yourself:** Take the time to learn about the support services and resources available via your organization. Familiarise yourself with the programs, benefits, and policies that may apply to your needs or ambitions.
- **Initiate Conversations:** Do not be reluctant to talk to your boss, HR department, or coworkers about your wants or issues. Seek assistance and advice on how to use the support services that are available to you.
- **Develop Relationships:** Connect with mentors, coaches, or colleagues who may offer advice, support, and encouragement as you traverse your personal or professional journey. When you need guidance or assistance, don't hesitate to ask.
- **Be Proactive:** Before requesting help, evaluate your needs, make goals, and advocate for yourself. Don't wait until you're in a crisis to seek assistance; instead, reach out early and regularly to address possible concerns before they worsen.
- **Utilise Available Resources:** Take advantage of the resources and programs that are available to you, such as counseling services, professional development opportunities, and financial aid programs. If the initial resources you seek are insufficient, don't be afraid to seek assistance or look into other options.

- **Seek input:** Request input from superiors, mentors, or coworkers about your performance, goals, and areas for development. This input can help you find potential for growth and development, as well as influence your efforts to seek organisational assistance.
- **Be Persistent:** Even if you face hurdles or setbacks along the path, remain determined to get the assistance you require. Don't give up if your first attempts are unsuccessful; keep advocating for yourself and exploring alternate possibilities until you obtain the support you need.

# 11

# CHAPTER TEN: LONG-TERM STRATEGIES AND PREVENTION

## Stress Prevention Technique

Stress prevention entails taking proactive measures to lessen the likelihood of stress-related problems before they arise. Rather than waiting until stress becomes excessive, preventative strategies focus on building resilience, controlling potential stressors, and promoting a healthy lifestyle to reduce stress's influence on our lives. By implementing stress-reduction tactics into our daily routines, we may improve our emotional well-being, improve our ability to deal with problems and live a more fulfilling life.

## The Value of Stress Prevention

1. **Promotes Overall Well-Being:** Stress prevention approaches improve overall well-being by addressing the underlying causes of stress and developing resilience to better manage life's difficulties. Individuals who take proactive actions to alleviate stress can have improved physical health, mental clarity, and emotional stability.

2. **Reduces the risk of stress-related illnesses:** Chronic stress has been related to a variety of physical and mental health issues, including cardiovascular disease, diabetes, anxiety, and depression. Individuals who minimize stress before it becomes chronic or overwhelming can lower their chance of acquiring stress-related disorders and retain optimal health.

3. **Improves Coping abilities:** Stress management approaches to assist individuals in developing good coping abilities to deal with life's ups and downs. Individuals who learn how to manage stress in healthy ways can develop resilience, adaptability, and problem-solving skills that will benefit them in many aspects of their lives.

4. **Improves Relationships:** Chronic stress can strain relationships, causing conflict, resentment, and communication failures. Individuals who avoid stress and maintain emotional balance can build healthier, more rewarding relationships with their partners, family members, and friends.

5. **Boosts Productivity and Creativity:** High levels of stress can impair cognitive function, creativity, and productivity, making it difficult to focus, think clearly, and perform optimally. Individuals who avoid stress and promote relaxation can improve their cognitive ability, creativity, and productivity in both personal and professional interests.

## Common Sources of Stress

- **job Stress:** Deadlines, demanding workloads and interpersonal issues can all lead to job stress. Job uncertainty, long hours, and a lack of control over job activities can all hurt an employee's mental and emotional health.
- **Financial worry:** Financial concerns such as debt, unemployment, or future uncertainty can generate a great deal of worry and anxiety. Concerns about paying bills, preparing for retirement, or providing for family members can cause individuals and families to feel stressed out all the time.
- **Relationship Stress:** Conflicts, family responsibilities, and caregiving chores can all lead to stress in personal relationships. Communication

issues, a lack of support, and arguments about finances or parenting can strain relationships and raise stress levels.

- **Health-related Stress:** Chronic disease, injury, or disability can create significant stress and disturbance in people's lives. Managing symptoms, navigating the healthcare system, and dealing with the emotional toll of disease can be difficult and stressful.
- **Life Transitions:** Moving, beginning a new career, getting married, or having a baby can all be stressful and daunting. Adapting to change, dealing with uncertainty, and juggling various obligations can all contribute to increased stress during transitional times.

## Practical Stress Prevention Techniques

- **Mindfulness Meditation:** Mindfulness meditation is the practice of paying attention to the present moment with openness, curiosity, and acceptance. Mindfulness meditation can help people reduce stress, develop self-awareness, and build an inner sense of peace and tranquility.
- **Deep Breathing Exercises:** Deep breathing exercises can assist activate the body's relaxation response, which reduces stress and promotes calm. Individuals can relieve tension, worry, and stress by breathing slowly and deeply and focusing on the sensation of the breath.
- **Physical Exercise:** Regular physical activity is an effective stress reliever, generating endorphins and lowering cortisol levels. Walking, jogging, yoga, or dancing can help people relax, enhance their mood, and gain vitality.
- **Healthy Lifestyle Habits:** Practicing healthy lifestyle habits such as eating a balanced diet, getting adequate sleep, and avoiding excessive alcohol and caffeine can improve general well-being and reduce stress. Prioritizing self-care activities like relaxation, hobbies, and social contacts can also help people recharge and renew.
- **Time Management:** Effective time management can help people minimize stress by prioritizing work, setting realistic goals, and avoiding procrastination. Individuals can avoid stress and retain a feeling of balance in

their lives by breaking down work into smaller, more achievable steps and making time for self-care and relaxation.

- **Social Support:** Making strong social connections and seeking aid from friends, family, or support groups can help people cope with stress and adversity. Sharing problems, seeking advice, and receiving emotional support from others can help you find solace and perspective during stressful situations.

- **Cognitive Restructuring:** Cognitive restructuring is confronting problematic thought patterns and replacing them with more positive, realistic alternatives. Identifying and reframing skewed thinking can help people reduce anxiety, increase mood, and build resilience in the face of stress.

- **Relaxation Techniques:** Including relaxation techniques like progressive muscle relaxation, guided imagery, or aromatherapy in everyday routines can help people unwind, reduce stress, and relax. Experimenting with various strategies can help people determine what works best for them.

- **Setting Boundaries:** Establishing boundaries in personal and professional interactions is critical for reducing stress and establishing healthy boundaries. Individuals can avoid burnout, and conflict, and maintain their well-being by assertively communicating their needs, priorities, and limitations.

- **Seeking Professional Help:** In some circumstances, stress can become overpowering or chronic, necessitating professional assistance. Seeking help from a therapist, counsellor, or healthcare provider can provide people with the tools, resources, and direction they need to address underlying issues, build coping techniques, and recover control of their life.

## Benefits of Using Stress Prevention Techniques

1. **Improved Physical Health:** Lowering stress levels can reduce the likelihood of stress-related illnesses while also improving overall physical health and well-being.

2. **Enhanced Mental Health:** Stress prevention practices increase emotional

resilience, minimize anxiety and depression symptoms, and improve general mental health and well-being.

3. **Increased Productivity and Performance:** By efficiently managing stress, people can increase their concentration, focus, and productivity, resulting in more success and happiness in personal and professional pursuits.

4. **Better Relationships:** By reducing stress and encouraging relaxation, people can increase communication, empathy, and connection in their relationships, resulting in more harmony and happiness.

5. **Enhanced Quality of Life:** Finally, adopting stress-reduction tactics into everyday routines can result in a higher quality of life, increased resilience, and a stronger sense of general well-being and fulfillment.

# Building Resilience

Resilience is commonly defined as the ability to withstand and recover from adversity, setbacks, and obstacles. It is not about avoiding unpleasant events or downplaying their significance, but about confronting them full-on, adjusting to change, and learning and developing from the experience. Resilience is a dynamic process that involves using inner strengths, social support, and coping skills to traverse life's unavoidable ups and downs with courage, tenacity, and adaptability.

## The Importance of Resilience

1. **Improves Mental and Emotional Well-Being:** Resilience is strongly related to mental and emotional well-being, as it helps people deal with stress, worry, and despair. Individuals who cultivate resilience can develop inner resources and coping abilities, allowing them to better manage life's hardships and maintain a positive view.

2. **Promotes Physical Health:** According to research, resilient people have superior physical health results, such as fewer chronic illnesses, faster recovery from illness or accident, and a longer life expectancy. Resilience

can improve physical health and well-being by lowering stress and encouraging appropriate coping methods.

3. **Encourages adaptability and flexibility:** In today's fast-changing environment, adaptability and flexibility are critical abilities for success. Individuals with resilience may embrace change, overcome ambiguity, and thrive in dynamic circumstances by cultivating a curious, open, and experimentative mindset.

4. **Strengthens Relationships:** Resilient people have stronger, more supportive relationships with their families, friends, and coworkers. Resilient people can create deeper relationships and weather relationship obstacles more effectively if they can communicate effectively, express their feelings, and seek help when necessary.

5. **Promotes Personal Growth and Development:** Adversity can be a catalyst for human growth and development by encouraging resilience and self-discovery. Resilient people can gain new abilities, strengths, and views that will benefit them in all aspects of their lives by tackling obstacles, learning from mistakes, and seizing opportunities for progress.

## Characteristics of Resilient Individuals

- **Optimism and Positive Outlook:** Resilient people keep a positive attitude towards life, even in the face of hardship. They focus on what they can alter rather than what they cannot, and they face obstacles with hope and optimism.

- **A.daptability and Flexibility:** Resilient people are adaptable and flexible, able to change their plans, goals, and expectations based on changing circumstances. They see change as an opportunity for growth and learning, rather than a danger.

- **Sense of Purpose and Meaning:** Resilient people have a clear sense of purpose and meaning in their lives, which gives them direction and motivation throughout challenging times. They may discover purpose and significance in their experiences, even in the face of adversity.

- **Social Support and Connection:** Resilient people have strong networks of family, friends, and community members. They seek assistance when necessary, give assistance to others, and cultivate positive relationships that provide comfort, encouragement, and strength.

- **Problem-Solving Skills:** Resilient people are competent problem solvers who can identify solutions, take decisive action, and persevere in the face of setbacks. They face obstacles with resourcefulness, inventiveness, and tenacity, looking for opportunities to grow and learn.

## Practical Strategies for Building Resilience.

- **Cultivate Self-awareness:** Self-awareness is the first step in developing resilience; it involves understanding your strengths, shortcomings, and coping methods. Take the time to consider your thoughts, feelings, and behaviors, and discover areas for improvement and development.
- **Develop Coping Skills:** Develop healthy coping skills to deal with stress, worry, and other tough emotions. Deep breathing, meditation, and progressive muscle relaxation are among the relaxation practices that can help you quiet your mind and body during stressful situations.
- **Create Social Support Networks:** Develop strong relationships with family, friends, and coworkers who can offer encouragement, wisdom, and support during challenging times. When assistance is required, seek it and, in turn, aid others.
- **Maintain a Positive Outlook:** Choose to focus on your strengths, accomplishments, and blessings rather than concentrating on negative thoughts or setbacks. To increase resilience and well-being, cultivate thankfulness, optimism, and self-compassion.
- **Set Realistic objectives:** Establish realistic objectives and expectations for yourself, breaking down larger ambitions into smaller, more doable ones. Focus on what you can control rather than what is beyond your control, and enjoy your progress along the way.
- **Embrace Change:** Change is a normal element of life that provides opportunities for growth and learning. Be receptive to new experiences, challenges, and possibilities, and approach change with curiosity, adapt-

ability, and resilience.

- **Seek Meaning and Purpose:** Make sense of your experiences, especially if they are painful. Focus on your values, passions, and ambitions, and look for chances for growth, connection, and contribution that are consistent with your sense of purpose.

- **Self-care:** Prioritise activities that nourish your mind, body, and soul, such as exercise, a healthy diet, enough sleep, and leisure activities. Take time to rest and rejuvenate, and pay attention to your body's cues to avoid burnout and tiredness.

- **Learn from Adversity:** See adversity as a learning opportunity and a chance to build resilience and strength. Reflect on previous trials and defeats, identify lessons learned, and apply those insights to guide your approach to future issues.

- **Seek expert Help:** If you're having trouble coping with stress or misfortune, don't be afraid to seek assistance from a therapist, counsellor, or mental health expert. They can offer assistance, advice, and methods to help you develop resilience and navigate challenging circumstances.

## Benefits of Developing Resilience

- **Greater Emotional Well-being:** Cultivating resilience enhances emotional well-being, allowing people to better cope with stress, anxiety, and despair.

- **Improved Problem-Solving Skills:** Resilient people have great problem-solving abilities, allowing them to overcome challenges and obstacles with creativity, resourcefulness, and determination.

- **Enhanced Adaptation and Flexibility:** Resilience promotes adaptation and flexibility, allowing people to accept change, navigate ambiguity, and thrive in dynamic circumstances.

- **Stronger Relationships:** Resilient people have stronger, more supportive relationships with their families, friends, and colleagues, which leads to a higher sense of connection and happiness in both their personal and professional lives.

- **Increased Confidence and Self-esteem:** Building resilience increases confidence and self-esteem, allowing people to overcome difficulties, take chances, and pursue their dreams with courage and persistence.
- **Improved Physical Health:** Resilient people have superior physical health outcomes, such as fewer chronic illnesses, faster recovery from illness or accident, and a longer lifespan.
- **Greater Sense of Purpose and Meaning:** Cultivating resilience helps people discover meaning and purpose in their experiences, which fosters a sense of direction, motivation, and fulfillment in life.

# Holistic Well-being Approaches

Holistic well-being is a multifaceted notion that includes the physical, mental, emotional, and spiritual components of health and wellness. Rather than focusing merely on the absence of illness or disease, holistic well-being emphasizes the necessity of finding balance, harmony, and vitality in all aspects of life. It acknowledges that each human is complex and interrelated being shaped by a variety of elements such as heredity, environment, lifestyle, and personal ideas and values.

The concept that optimal health and happiness can only be obtained by integrating mind, body, and spirit is central to holistic well-being. This holistic approach recognizes that physical health is inextricably linked to mental and emotional well-being and that spiritual fulfillment is required for overall pleasure and fulfillment. Holistic well-being approaches seek to enhance health, happiness, and vitality from within by addressing the needs of the entire individual - body, mind, and spirit.

## Key Elements of Holistic Well-Being

**1. Physical Well-being:** Physical well-being refers to the health and vitality of the body, which includes factors such as nutrition, exercise, sleep, and preventive care. It entails developing healthy lifestyle habits that promote physical health and longevity, including eating a balanced diet, engaging in regular physical activity, obtaining enough sleep, and abstaining from dangerous substances such as tobacco and excessive alcohol.

**2. Mental Wellbeing:** Mental well-being refers to the state and function of the mind, which includes cognitive function, emotional regulation, and psychological resilience. Mindfulness meditation, cognitive-behavioral therapy, and relaxation techniques are among the activities used to increase mental clarity, emotional stability, and stress reduction.

**3. Emotional Well-being:** Emotional well-being is the ability to understand, express, and manage one's emotions healthily and constructively. It includes self-awareness, empathy, and emotional resilience, as well as activities that encourage self-care, self-compassion, and positive connections.

**4. Spiritual Well-being:** Spiritual well-being refers to a sense of connection, purpose, and meaning in life, which includes personal values, beliefs, and a sense of identity. Meditation, prayer, introspection, and acts of kindness and compassion are all practices that promote spiritual growth.

## Practical Strategies for Holistic Well-Being

1. **Mindful Eating:** Practice mindful eating by focusing on the sensory experiences of eating, such as taste, texture, and smell. Eat carefully, enjoy each bite, and pay attention to your body's hunger and fullness signs. Choose full, nutrient-dense foods that will fuel your body and promote overall health and well-being.
2. **Regular Exercise:** Engage in enjoyable physical activities such as walking, jogging, swimming, yoga, or dance. To promote cardiovascular health, muscular strength, and flexibility, combine aerobic activity with strength training and flexibility exercises.
3. **Quality Sleep:** Prioritize sleep by setting a consistent sleep schedule and a pleasant nighttime routine. Aim for seven to nine hours of sleep per

night, and create a sleeping environment that is dark, quiet, and pleasant. Avoid using electronic gadgets, and coffee, and engage in stimulating activities before bedtime.

4. **Stress Management:** To relieve stress and increase relaxation, use techniques like deep breathing, progressive muscle relaxation, and mindfulness meditation. Take regular breaks during the day to rest and recharge, and do things that make you happy and fulfilled.

5. **Emotional Expression:** Express your feelings in healthy and productive ways, such as journaling, talking with a trusted friend or therapist, or participating in creative activities such as art, music, or dancing. Allow yourself to feel the whole range of emotions without judgment or suppression.

6. **Cultivate ties:** Develop positive ties with family, friends, and community people who encourage and motivate you. Make time for meaningful connections and shared experiences, and be open and honest with others about your views, feelings, and needs.

7. **Mindfulness Practice:** Incorporate mindfulness techniques into your daily routine, such as mindfulness meditation, attentive breathing, and mindful movement. Take the time to be present in the moment, free of judgment or distractions, and nurture inner serenity and calm.

8. **Spiritual Connection:** Develop a sense of spiritual connection and purpose by engaging in practices that nourish your soul and enhance your connection to something bigger than yourself. This could involve prayer, meditation, nature hikes, or acts of service and compassion.

9. **Gratitude Practice:** Every day, reflect on what you are grateful for. Maintain a thankfulness book or simply take a few moments each day to express gratitude for the benefits in your life, large and small.

10. **Self-care Rituals:** Make self-care a priority by introducing regular rituals into your daily routine. This can involve taking a warm bath, doing moderate yoga, drinking herbal tea, or engaging in a favorite hobby or activity that provides you joy and relaxation.

## Benefits of Holistic Wellness Approaches

- **Improved Physical Health:** Holistic well-being approaches improve total physical health and vitality, which lowers the risk of chronic illness and increases longevity.
- **Enhanced Mental and Emotional Well-Being:** By addressing the interdependence of mind, body, and spirit, holistic well-being techniques promote mental clarity, emotional stability, and psychological resilience.
- **Greater Resilience and Adaptation:** Holistic well-being techniques encourage resilience and adaptation, allowing people to face life's obstacles with strength, grace, and flexibility.
- **Deeper Sense of Fulfilment:** Holistic well-being approaches foster a sense of purpose, meaning, and connection in life, resulting in a greater sense of fulfillment and happiness.
- **Improved connections:** Holistic well-being approaches promote healthy connections and communication skills, resulting in deeper connection and closeness in both personal and professional interactions.
- **Enhanced Quality of Life:** Ultimately, holistic well-being techniques result in a higher quality of life, as evidenced by increased balance, harmony, and vitality in all aspects of life.

# 12

# CONCLUSION

I n this book, we've taken a thorough look at stress and how to manage it. By deconstructing its numerous forms, understanding its origins, recognizing its symptoms, and digging into an arsenal of coping methods, we've given ourselves the tools we need to face life's unavoidable challenges with fortitude and grace.

From acute to chronic stress, and environmental stressors to cognitive-behavioral techniques, we've covered a wide range of strategies designed to address all aspects of the stress experience. We've learned to regain control of our health and build a greater sense of balance in our lives by incorporating relaxation techniques, mindfulness practices, and lifestyle changes.

Throughout this journey, one common theme has emerged: empowerment. Empowerment to identify indicators of stress in ourselves and others. Empowerment to take proactive steps to lessen the impact. Empowerment to seek help when necessary and prioritize self-care without guilt or hesitation.

As we wrap up our research, keep in mind that stress management is a continuous process of self-discovery and personal improvement. By incorporating the thoughts and strategies from this book into our daily lives, we can achieve more resilience, well-being, and fulfillment.

So, as you negotiate the intricacies of life, may you be equipped with the wisdom and empowerment to tackle stress full-on, knowing that every difficulty presents a chance for growth and change. Here's to your ongoing path toward a life of balance, resilience, and inner peace

116

www.ingramcontent.com/pod-product-compliance
Lightning Source LLC
Chambersburg PA
CBHW051817250726
48659CB00005B/1532